W9-BEX-581

ABRAHAM JOSHUA HESCHEL

Exploring His Life and Thought

BM
755
.H37
A27

ABRAHAM JOSHUA HESCHEL

Exploring His Life and Thought.

Edited and Introduced
by
JOHN C. MERKLE

MACMILLAN PUBLISHING COMPANY
A Division of Macmillan, Inc.
NEW YORK

Collier Macmillan Publishers
LONDON

Copyright © 1985 by Macmillan Publishing Company
A Division of Macmillan, Inc.

Copyright © 1985 by Samuel H. Dresner

All rights reserved. No part of this book may be reproduced or
transmitted in any form or by any means, electronic or mechanical,
including photocopying, recording, or by any information storage
and retrieval system, without permission in writing from the
Publisher.

Macmillan Publishing Company
A Division of Macmillan, Inc.
866 Third Avenue, New York, N. Y. 10022

Collier Macmillan Canada, Inc.

Library of Congress Catalog Card Number: 85-3086

Printed in the United States of America

printing number
1 2 3 4 5 6 7 8 9 10

Library of Congress Cataloging in Publication Data

Main entry under title:

Abraham Joshua Heschel : exploring his life and thought.

Based on presentations made at the Symposium on the
Life and Thought of Abraham Joshua Heschel, held May 9-11,
1983 at the College of Saint Benedict, St. Joseph, Minn.
Includes index.
1. Heschel, Abraham Joshua, 1907-1972—Congresses.
2. Scholars, Jewish—United States—Biography—
Congresses. 3. Judaism—Doctrines—Congresses. I. Merkle,
John C. II. Symposium on the Life and Thought of
Abraham Joshua Heschel (1983 : Saint Joseph, Minn.)
BM755.H34A27 1985 296.3'092'4 85-3086
ISBN 0-02-920970-6

Contents

PART THREE
HESCHEL AS PHILOSOPHER AND POET

PART FOUR
HESCHEL AS SOCIAL CRITIC AND ECUMENIST

Acknowledgments

The College of Saint Benedict sponsored and hosted the Symposium on the Life and Thought of Abraham Joshua Heschel that gave rise to this book. So many persons from its faculty, staff, and student body contributed to the symposium's success that they cannot all be mentioned here. I trust that they know of my heartfelt gratitude to them.

Sister Emmanuel Renner, O.S.B., President of the College of Saint Benedict; Sister Colman O'Connell, O.S.B., Executive Vice-President of our college; and Sister Linda Kulzer, O.S.B., our Vice-President for Academic Affairs, deserve special mention for their encouragement and support of the symposium from the very moment it was conceived as an idea.

My colleagues in the Theology Department—and our secretary, Maxine Andraschko, who typed the manuscript of this book—were particularly helpful along the way. Ed Adleson, who organized and directed the symposium concerts, and his colleagues and the students in the Music Department, immeasurably enhanced the grandeur of the event. Charles Dewey helped create the symposium brochure and did a lovely drawing of Heschel included within it. Sister Cecelia Prokosh, O.S.B., and her staff kashered the kitchens and prepared and served kosher meals for all the symposium participants and members of the local community who dined at the convent and college during the symposium; they thereby helped to make the symposium a truly ecumenical event where all could feel comfortably at home.

My gratitude extends to those from beyond our college who helped make the symposium a success: to the speakers whose names and papers appear in this volume, to Rabbi Hershel Matt who prepared and led a moving prayer service, to Rabbi Nahum Schulman who supervised the kashering of the kitchen and was the master of ceremonies at the symposium banquet, to composers John Ware and Neale Powell Lundgren who contributed works in memory of Heschel that were performed here, to the musicians who joined members of our own Music Department and performed so beautifully, to Corita Kent who did the magnificent painting and design for the symposium poster and brochure cover, and to the Gelco Corporation and the Minnesota Humanities Commission in cooperation with the National Endowment for the Humanities for their generous donations to the College of Saint Benedict toward the funding of the symposium.

Finally, I am grateful to all who came from near and far across this country to participate in the symposium and helped to make it a scholarly, ecumenical, and spiritual event of great significance.

JOHN C. MERKLE
College of Saint Benedict
St. Joseph, Minnesota

About The Contributors

BERNHARD W. ANDERSON PH.D., D.D., S.T.D. Professor Emeritus of Old Testament Theology at Princeton Theological Seminary, Dr. Anderson is one of the most respected biblical scholars in the United States. A prolific author, he is most well known for *Understanding the Old Testament*. Among his other books are: *The Unfolding Drama of the Bible* and *The Living Word of the Bible*. Included among his numerous articles are significant contributions to *The Interpreter's Dictionary of the Bible*. Dr. Anderson has also served as Dean of the Theological School at Drew University and as President of the Society of Biblical Literature.

ROBERT MCAFEE BROWN, PH.D. Professor of Theology and Ethics at Pacific School of Religion, Berkeley, Dr. Brown is one of the most renowned theologians in the United States. He has written more than 20 books, one of which he co-authored with Rabbi Heschel: *Vietnam: Crisis of Conscience*. Among his other works are: *Religion and Violence, Is Faith Obsolete?*, and *Theology in a New Key*. Dr. Brown represented the World Alliance of Presbyterian and Reformed Churches as Protestant Observer at the Second Vatican Council and is a member of the United States Holocaust Memorial Council.

SAMUEL H. DRESNER, D.H.L. Rabbi Dresner, who has served as rabbi of the Moriah Congregation in Deerfield, Illinois, and as Adjunct Professor of Jewish Thought at Spertus College, Chicago, did his doctoral studies and dissertation under Rabbi Heschel's guidance at the Jewish Theological Seminary of America. He is the author of numerous articles and books, including *Prayer, Humility, and Compassion* and *The Sabbath*. He has recently edited two works entitled *I Asked for Wonder: A Spiritual Anthology from the Writings of Abraham J. Heschel*, and *The Circle of the Baal Shem Tov: Studies in Hasidism*, essays by Abraham J. Heschel.

EVA FLEISCHNER, PH.D. Professor of Religion at Montclair State College, New Jersey, Dr. Fleischner is prominent in the field of Jewish-Christian relations. Her articles have appeared in a variety of journals and she is the author and editor of two important books in this area: *The View of Judaism in German Christian Theology since 1945* and *Auschwitz: Beginning of a New Era?*, a volume of papers delivered at the International Symposium on the Holocaust at the Cathedral of St. John the Divine in New York City, 1974. Dr. Fleischner serves on the advisory boards of the Office of Christian-Jewish Relations of the National Council of Churches and the Office of Catholic-Jewish Relations of the United States Bishops' Catholic Conference.

EDWARD K. KAPLAN, PH.D. Associate Professor of French at Brandeis University, Dr. Kaplan is the author of *Michelet's Poetic Vision: A Romantic Philosophy of Nature, Man, and Woman.* He was deeply influenced by Heschel and for several years taught a course entitled "Mysticism and the Moral Life" at Amherst College. He has published articles on the French writers, Nerval, Hugo, Baudelaire, Rimbaud, Michelet, and Bachelard, and on the religious thinkers, Buber, Merton, Thurman, and Heschel. His most recent book is *Mother Death: The Journal of Jules Michelet, 1815–50,* and he is now writing a book on the poetry of Baudelaire.

WOLFE KELMAN, D.D. The Executive Vice President of The Rabbinical Assembly since 1951, Rabbi Kelman has also been President of the Hebrew Arts Foundation and Chairman of Cultural Commission of the World Jewish Congress. He has taught history and homiletics at Jewish Theological Seminary of America. A close personal friend of Rabbi Heschel's for many years, Rabbi Kelman delivered the eulogy at Heschel's funeral.

JOHN C. MERKLE, PH.D. Dr. Merkle is Assistant Professor of Theology at the College of Saint Benedict, St. Joseph, Minnesota. He did his doctoral studies at the Catholic University of Louvain (K.U.L.), Belgium, where his dissertation focused on the thought of Rabbi Heschel. His book, entitled *The Genesis of Faith: The Depth Theology of Abraham Joshua Heschel* was published by Macmillan Publishing Company in 1985. Dr. Merkle has had a variety of articles on Heschel published in scholarly journals in the United States, Canada, Central America, and Europe. He conceived and directed the national symposium on Heschel, the proceedings of which form the content of this book.

URSULA M. NIEBUHR, D.D. Educated in history and theology at Oxford University, Dr. Niebuhr taught in the Department of Religion at Barnard College in New York City for 25 years. A distinguished scholar herself, she worked with her late husband, Reinhold Niebuhr, perhaps the most influential American Protestant theologian of the twentieth century. Active in Jewish-Christian dialogue, Dr. Niebuhr has been Scholar in Residence at The Ecumenical Institute for Advanced Theological Studies at Tantur, Israel.

FRITZ A. ROTHSCHILD, D.H.L. Dr. Rothschild is Associate Professor of Religion and Chairman of the Department of Jewish Philosophy at Jewish Theological Seminary of America. A former student and colleague of Rabbi Heschel's, since the 1950s he has been recognized by the scholarly community as the most authoritative interpreter of Heschel's thought. Along with several scholarly articles on Heschel, Dr. Rothschild has edited and introduced *Between God and Man: An Interpretation of Judaism from the Writings of Abraham J. Heschel.*

Introduction

JOHN C. MERKLE

The essays in this book were first presented as lectures at the Symposium on the Life and Thought of Abraham Joshua Heschel at the College of Saint Benedict, St. Joseph, Minnesota, May 9–11, 1983. Commemorating the tenth anniversary of Rabbi Heschel's death (December 23, 1972), the symposium featured lectures on various aspects of his thought and reminiscences about him by those who knew him well. There were also two concerts, a banquet, and a prayer service in memory of Heschel, at which his widow, Sylvia Heschel, and daughter, Susannah, were guests of honor.

The speakers included Jewish, Protestant, and Catholic scholars in various disciplines from throughout the United States. Numerous other scholars were among the participants who came from near and far. Some 130 women and men from across this country joined hundreds of teachers and students from the local college community to explore some of Heschel's principal teachings and scholarly contributions, to learn more about his life, and to honor his memory.

Rabbi Heschel was one of America's most prophetic religious leaders and perhaps the foremost Jewish religious thinker of the twentieth century. Reinhold Niebuhr expressed the thoughts of many people when he described Heschel as "the most authentic prophet of religious life in our culture."[1] And many of us agree with Will Herberg in regarding Heschel as "the most significant Jewish religious thinker of our day in America."[2] However, despite such acclaim, Heschel's biography is yet to be written, and his contributions to religious studies have not received the scholarly attention they deserve. Like the symposium whose offspring it is, this book is meant to help remedy this situation—by its biographical content and by the scholarly attention it contains and hopes to inspire.

However, the significance of the symposium was not primarily academic, but rather spiritual and ecumenical. This, of course, is as it should have been with a symposium on Heschel, whose scholarship was a sacred art in the service of God and a creative exploration of the religious sensitivities and insights that unite men and women of different religious traditions. In the midst of this academic adventure, Jews and Christians became convinced that the things that divide us are less real than the spirit that unites us. What could have pleased Heschel more? Was there anyone who reminded us more than Heschel did of how very much we need each other and of our shared humanity before the divine? Who more than Heschel knew that, despite our differences in doctrine and religious practice, we are really one in faith—in our faith in the God of Abraham. What Heschel proposed as the basis of interreligious dialogue was not merely intellectually perceived, but spiritually sensed at this symposium. Heschel once said:

> I suggest that the most significant basis for meeting of men and women of different religious traditions is the level of fear and trembling, of humility and contrition, where our individual moments of faith are mere waves in the endless ocean of mankind's reaching out for God, where all formulations and articulations appear as understatements, where our souls are swept away by the awareness of the urgency of answering God's commandment, while stripped of pretension and conceit we sense the tragic insufficiency of human faith. . . . The purpose of religious communication among human beings of different commitments is mutual enrichment and enhancement of respect and appreciation. . . . It is neither to flatter nor to refute one another, but to help one another; to share insight and learning, to cooperate in academic ventures on the highest scholarly level, and what is even more important, to search in the wilderness for well-springs of devotion, for treasures of stillness, for the power of love and care . . . , to cooperate in trying to bring about a resurrection of sensitivity, a revival of conscience, and faithfulness to the Living God.[3]

This vision of Heschel's was momentarily realized at the symposium, which Fritz Rothschild has described as a "spiritual adventure, a truly historic and memorable event of sharing between Catholics, Protestants, and Jews in a warm and loving fellowship where we were all enriched, stimulated, and educated."[4]

The spiritual quality of the symposium was enhanced in no small measure by the sublime music of the two concerts. Several musicians from the Chicago Symphony Orchestra, the Minnesota Orchestra, the St. Paul Chamber Orchestra, and faculty members from the College of Saint Benedict and two neighboring schools—St. John's University and St. Cloud State University—were featured along with an orchestra comprised of students from the three local colleges. One of the pieces performed was John Ware's "Deploration for String Orchestra on the Death of Rabbi A. J. Heschel," composed in 1973. Concerning the circumstances of the composition, Ware wrote:

> Rabbi Heschel visited Superior, Wisconsin, when I was teaching there; he was the commencement speaker for the winter graduation ceremonies for the College of Saint Scholastica, Duluth. Since CSS had no large auditorium, the ceremony was held at the University of Wisconsin–Superior. The UWS Music Department provided both choral and orchestral music for the occasion (I played in the orchestra). The address given by Rabbi Heschel was of such singular beauty and so moved the audience that he was deeply loved and admired by an audience which would otherwise never have heard of him. We were all shocked at his death about a month later, and several faculty members at both UWS and College of St. Scholastica produced memorial tributes. My own work was begun almost immediately after I learned of his death (in January 1973) and was finished in about six weeks. The work was first used at the dedication of the new Fine Arts Building at UWS, which was considered fitting since Rabbi Heschel's address had been the last major event in the old facility.[5]

Ware's words are indicative of how Heschel affected the countless audiences before which he spoke, in this nation and beyond. The audiences at the symposium concerts were similarly touched by the beautiful performances in memory of Heschel.

It was only appropriate to include music in the symposium since Heschel once claimed that "the shattering experience of music has been a challenge to my thinking on ultimate issues" and that "the only language that seems to be compatible with the wonder and mystery of being is the language of music."[6] More than lectures alone could have done, the concerts helped the symposium attain a level of grandeur compatible with the poetic language of Heschel's inspired teachings.

Also contributing to the spiritual atmosphere of the symposium were the kosher meals provided by the sisters from St. Benedict's Convent. Supervised by an Orthodox rabbi, Nahum Schulman, the convent and college kitchens were kashered several days before the symposium began. Not only the symposium participants from outside the college, but also the nearly 2,000 sisters, students, and faculty who dined at the convent and college during the symposium partook of kosher meals. (Perhaps a "first" on so large a scale at a Christian institution?) The St. Benedict's community knew and appreciated the fact that something unique—something holy—was happening during these days.

The prayer service, prepared and presided over by Rabbi Hershel Matt, contributed further to the spiritual and ecumenical significance of the symposium. A student of Heschel's who has made contributions to the field of ecumenism, Rabbi Matt conducted a service befitting the memory of a man whose writings about prayer are as deep and penetrating as can be found. Adding to the sublimity of the occasion was a song entitled "Who Lit the Wonder?"—with words taken from a text of Heschel's—composed for the service by Neale Powell Lundgren.

The lectures, too, were not merely academic in nature, but contributed to the ecumenical and spiritual climate of the event. The mood of the entire symposium was captured in words by Susannah Heschel in a letter written shortly afterwards:

> I was amazed at the participation—so many people from such different backgrounds, from all parts of the country. Everything went so smoothly—all the lectures, meals, concerts, housing. But most precious of all was the atmosphere, the mood in which the whole symposium took place. In Hasidism, every gesture is supposed to be accompanied by the proper kavana, intention. That was what I experienced at St. Benedict's—from the guest house to the dining room to the posters to the introductions of the speakers. I became aware that new depths of meaning appeared for me in the quotations from my father's works that were read by the speakers—even though I had heard the same words quoted many, many times in the past. The way a sentence was read, the kavana behind it, gave it new light. For that, I am especially grateful.[7]

The lectures themselves drew not only the 130 full-time participants from outside the college, but audiences ranging from approximately 350 to 1,000 listeners, a testimony to the impact Heschel had already made upon the faculty, the students, and others from the College of Saint Benedict and the local community. Prior to the symposium, hundreds of students and faculty here had read, studied, and discussed books and essays by Heschel.

There were three symposium addresses that were biographical in nature; they comprise the first part of this book. Rabbi Samuel Dresner's "Heschel the Man" is a penetrating look at the person behind the scholar. Rabbi Wolfe Kelman, who delivered the eulogy at Heschel's funeral, presents "A Tribute to Rabbi Heschel" more than a decade later. Dr. Ursula Niebuhr, in her "Notes on a Friendship," reflects for the first time in print on the relationship between Heschel and her late husband, Reinhold Niebuhr, perhaps the most influential American Protestant theologian of our time.

There were six symposium lectures that dealt with various aspects of Heschel's thought; they comprise the remainder of this book. The second part of the book focuses on Heschel as a biblical theologian. Professor Bernhard Anderson, himself a famous biblical scholar, examines Heschel's exposition of biblical theology under the title "Coexistence with God." In my own essay, "Heschel's Theology of Divine Pathos," I explore and defend what might be Heschel's most revolutionary doctrine.

The third part of the book deals with Heschel as a philosopher and a poet. Professor Fritz Rothschild, widely recognized as the most authoritative interpreter of Heschel's philosophy, examines the "Varieties of Heschelian Thought." Professor Edward Kaplan, the leading interpreter of Heschel's use of language, analyzes "Heschel's Poetics of Religious Thinking."

The fourth part of the book contains essays dealing with Heschel as a social critic and an ecumenist. Professor Robert McAfee Brown, himself a renowned ethicist, examines Heschel's social ethics under the title "Some are Guilty, All are Responsible." Professor Eva Fleischner, prominent in the field of Jewish-Christian relations, explores "Heschel's Significance for Jewish-Christian Reconciliation."

With the publication of this book, it is the hope of those of us who participated in the Heschel Symposium that its spirit will live on and touch the lives of those who read these pages.

Notes

1. Reinhold Niebuhr, quoted by Byron Sherwin, "Abraham Joshua Heschel," *The Torch* (Spring 1969), 5–8, p. 7.
2. Will Herberg, review of *The Natural and Supernatural Jew: An Historical and Theological Introduction* by Arthur Cohen, *Judaism,* 12 (Summer 1963), p. 365.
3. Abraham Joshua Heschel, "No Religion is an Island," *Union Seminary Quarterly Review,* 21 (January 1966), 117–134, pp. 122, 125–126, 133.

4. Fritz A. Rothschild, in a letter to Sister Emmanuel Renner, President, College of Saint Benedict, May 13, 1983.

5. John M. Ware, in a letter to Edward Adelson, Music Department, College of Saint Benedict, January 3, 1983.

6. Abraham Joshua Heschel, *The Insecurity of Freedom: Essays on Human Existence* (New York: Shocken Books, 1966), pp. 246, 245.

7. Susannah Heschel, in a letter to John C. Merkle, Theology Department, College of Saint Benedict, May 16, 1983.

PART
ONE

Remembering Abraham Joshua Heschel

1

Heschel the Man

SAMUEL H. DRESNER

Among the celebrations of the life and thought of Rabbi Abraham Joshua Heschel on the tenth anniversary of his passing, this is surely the grandest and the most unusual. It is sponsored by those of another faith: Catholics have arranged this moving conference in honor of a Jew. And yet, how appropriate it is. For the Jew here honored inspired people of many faiths, and he labored tirelessly to enhance the relationship between Church and Synagogue. And how right it is, in a period of divine eclipse, that Jews and Christians together focus on the life and work of someone upon whom God's light continued to shine. Indeed, in a time of such madness, when the earth threatens to explode in our hands, how else to preserve sanity than by recalling saints of old with whom to commune; by pouring over enlightened texts from which to regain insight; and, above all, by identifying one who faced the absurd and the demonic and yet triumphed: who dared speak, even sing, of the glory of God and the marvel of man, of divine grace and human compassion. We are here to ponder his thoughts, consider his ways, and celebrate his life. To remember Heschel is not only to honor him but to restore ourselves.

In some ways it would be easier to treat Heschel the philosopher, the biblical scholar, or even the poet, for then an area of investigation would be marked out and the printed word available for all to examine. To discuss Heschel the man, however, is another matter—

perhaps a more difficult matter. Not only his words, but his dreams, his deeds, his entire life now become the subject of inquiry. Inquiries such as this are fraught with danger today, because ours is an age of flaunting irreverence, when debunking has taken on all the trappings of a national sport, and historians revel in revealing the clay feet of the mightiest. Heschel himself once observed that "Suspect thy neighbor as thyself" had become the newly emended version of the commandment. Contemporary biographers, nurtured in this subversive view of humanity, tend to be skeptical of human dignity.

A major theme of Heschel's writings, however, was human grandeur and dignity. For this, we find no argument more compelling than his works. As a youth, he titled his first book of poems, *Der Shem hameforash: Mentsh,* that is, *Man, the Ineffable Name of God.* For our purpose, the question is not so much what he intended by his defense of human grandeur, as how Heschel's views were related to his own life. "My father," his daughter has testified, "was the kind of man he wrote about."[1] To what extent, and in what way, was Heschel related to his writings? At the conclusion of his first major work in English, *Man Is Not Alone,* is a chapter entitled "The Pious Man." Heschel's method was phenomenological—that is, in brief, descriptive. But whom was he describing? While he told me that his model was primarily his uncle, the Novominsker Rebbe,[2] and though he must have had others in mind as well, both ancient and contemporary, whose works he had mastered and whose lives he knew well, what of his own personal testimony? Could he have written the following passage, for example, without experiencing something of what he wrote?

> Awareness of God is as close to the pious man as the throbbing of his own heart, often deep and calm but at times overwhelming, intoxicating, setting the soul afire. The momentous reality of God stands there as peace, power, and endless tranquility, as an inexhaustible source of help, as boundless compassion, as an open gate awaiting prayer. It sometimes happens that the life of a pious man becomes so involved in God that his heart overflows as though it were a cup in the hand of God.[3]

One cannot properly understand Heschel the man without studying his thought. The obverse is also true: to properly understand Heschel's thought, one must examine his life.

Nasi: A Prince of His People

Who was Abraham Joshua Heschel?

If the sages of Talmud were correct in saying that Israel's teachers are its royalty, then Heschel, the preeminent Jewish teacher of our generation, was a *Nasi,* a prince of his people. Indeed, he was elected to high office as much by others as by his own.

The Catholics elected Heschel.

His pervasive influence was felt at Vatican Council II, which was to review Catholic–Jewish relations in the form of a schema on the Jews. Requested by Cardinal Bea to draw up a proposal, Heschel traveled to Rome several times, where he argued for the Church's acceptance of "the permanent preciousness of the Jewish people." As Dr. Fleischner will point out later in this symposium, Heschel's efforts at Vatican II were of enormous significance. Moreover, Heschel left a deep impression in Italy. He made a lecture tour there in conjunction with the Vatican; his books were translated into Italian, and he is, I believe, the only Jewish thinker to be quoted by a Pope in this century.[4] After Heschel's death, the Catholic publication, *America,* devoted an entire issue to his memory (March 10, 1973). A number of major studies on Heschel's thought have been written by Catholics, among which is the work of this symposium's director, John Merkle.[5] Surely this unprecedented conference is final testimony of the esteem of Catholics for Heschel.

Perhaps these two personal episodes will help to illustrate Heschel's relationship to the Catholic community:[6]

One afternoon Heschel told me that he had just received a delegation of nuns. Their order was considering whether or not to give up their formal, longer habit for shorter, less cumbersome clothing. "What did you advise?" I asked. "I told them that such a personal matter should be settled by themselves." "But what is your opinion?" I persisted. "I do not believe they should change," he replied. How unusual that the nuns should have come to him at all with such a question!

Once, while walking past St. Patrick's Cathedral, a Jew (Dr. Shlomo Noble of the YIVO) noticed in progress a protest against the war in Vietnam, where Cardinal Cooke had gone to support the military mission. While the Jew took a leaflet and put a few coins on the tray, the young boy who handed him the tract, looked at him, and then, trying to make contact, said hesitantly, "I know Rabbi Heschel."[7] That name bridged the gap between a Catholic boy and the Jewish world.

The Protestants also elected Heschel.

The most influential Protestant thinker in America in this century, Reinhold Niebuhr, placed Heschel for the first time before the American reading public when, in the Sunday *New York Herald Tribune Book Review* of April 1, 1951, he wrote: "Abraham Heschel is one of the treasuries of spirit by which the persecutions, unloosed in Europe, inadvertently enriched our American culture. . . . He will become a commanding and authoritative voice not only in the Jewish community but in the religious life of America."[8] Years later (1965-1966) Heschel became the first Jewish professor at The Union Theological Seminary in New York. Shortly after his death, I saw a handwritten letter on Heschel's desk from a noted Protestant which began with the salutation: "Dear Father Abraham!" And in his column in *The Christian Century,* Martin Marty wrote: "Has the death of anyone since Pope John moved us so much?"[9]

And the Muslims elected Heschel.

In 1972, some months before his death and against doctor's orders, Abraham Heschel attended a hitherto unpublicized conference in Rome. "It was the first occasion since the establishment of the State of Israel"—and the last—"that religious and other leaders of the three faiths involved in Jerusalem had met together to define the religious content of their devotion to the Holy City."[10] The conference had been proposed by the Anglican Archbishop of Jerusalem and was sponsored by the Center for Mediterranean Studies in Rome, in cooperation with the Friends and the Jerusalem Foundation, "to explore the religious dynamics of the Jerusalem problem by attempting to define the *spiritual* necessities embedded in each of the three religions involved with the city."[11] It was their hope that political considerations might be influenced by the "devout and profound personalities present."[12]

Archbishop Appleton opened each day's discussion with prayers, and a reading was given by each of the different faiths. Heschel was invited to read for the Jews. Observing that the coming Sabbath immediately preceded Rosh Hashana, the Jewish New Year, he recited the prophetical portion from Isaiah assigned for that Sabbath in the Synagogue liturgy:

For Zion's sake will I not hold my peace,
And for Jerusalem's sake I will not rest,
Until her triumph go forth as brightness,
And her salvation as a torch that burneth.
And the nations shall see thy triumph,
And all kings thy glory; . . .
Thou shalt no more be termed forsaken,
Neither shall thy land any more be termed desolate; . . .
For the Lord delighteth in thee,
And thy land shall be espoused. . . .
As the bridegroom rejoiceth over the bride,
So shall thy God rejoice over thee.
I have set watchmen upon thy walls, O Jerusalem,
They shall never hold their peace day nor night:
"Ye that are the Lord's remembrancers,
Take ye no rest, and give Him no rest,
Till He establish, and till He make Jerusalem
A praise in the earth. . . ."
For He said: "Surely, they are My people,
Children that will not deal falsely. . . ."
In all their affliction He was afflicted,
And the angel of His presence saved them;
And He bore them, and carried them all the days of old.
    (Isaiah 62: 1, 2, 4, 5–7; 63: 8–9)

After the ecumenical service had concluded, Heschel visibly moved the Muslims by remarking that, "It is important for me to remember now, that while I have prayed from the heart for the Muslims all my life, I have never prayed with them before, or been face-to-face with them to talk about God. This is *so* important. We must go further."[13]

Heschel believed that seemingly insoluble problems, even one so hoary and complex as Jerusalem, could be resolved if a spiritual understanding were first achieved. He trusted that even during those few meetings a "common language among the religions could be found."[14] Summarizing the conference, the Center director, E. A. Bayne, wrote:

In such a setting Rabbi Heschel performed superbly as we had hoped. Although fragile in health, his spirit never flagged. . . . Largely because of his presence, I believe, in support of the spiritual dimension of the inquiry, the seminar was rewarding. It was clear that theologically, at least, Muslim and Jew understood the holistic nature of their respective faiths—and the necessity, therefore, for compassion and compromise. Christians, themselves divided, seemed less comfortable in the discussion (it was they, for example, who expressed fear about the taping of the proceedings; neither the Muslims nor the Jewish contingent were concerned!). Had we had funds, however, another session could have been fruitful, if not definitive; but it was not to be.[16]

At the close of the final session, Heschel, who moved slowly in those days, shuffled toward the door with only the two Muslim Kahdis apparently remaining behind. One approached him, squeezed his hand and departed. The second took his hand and said: "I have read all that you have written. God bless your work."

The Blacks elected Heschel.

A picture which should hang in Black and Jewish homes is that of Heschel and Martin Luther King marching arm-in-arm in Selma, Alabama, an event Heschel recalled in typically striking summation: "When I marched in Selma, my feet were praying." Heschel and King not only marched together they had profound respect for each other as well. Shortly before King's assassination, Heschel said of him:

> Martin Luther King is a sign that God has not forsaken the United States of America. God has sent him to us. . . . His mission is sacred. . . . I call upon every Jew to hearken to his voice, to share his vision, to follow in his way. The whole future of America will depend upon the . . . influence of Dr. King.[17]

Describing Heschel as "one of the great men of our age, a truly great prophet," King recognized Heschel's contribution to the Civil Rights Movement:

> He has been with us in many struggles. I remember marching from Selma to Montgomery, how he stood at my side. . . . I remember very well when we were in Chicago for the Conference on Religion and Race. . . . To a great extent his speech inspired clergymen of all faiths . . . to do something that they had not done before.[18]

In that historic speech to which King referred, given in 1963 at the initial Conference on Religion and Race in Chicago, Heschel's opening words startled his audience and helped to set the stage for the momentous changes that were to come:

> At the first Conference on Religion and Race, the main participants were Pharaoh and Moses. Moses' words were: "Thus says the Lord, the God of Israel, let my people go that they may celebrate a feast to me." While Pharaoh retorted: "Who is the Lord that I should heed this voice and let Israel go? I do not know the Lord, and moreover I will not let Israel go."
>
> The outcome of that summit meeting has not come to an end. Pharaoh is not ready to capitulate. The exodus began, but is far from having been completed.[19]

By the 1970s the coalition of Blacks and Jews, which had worked so effectively and successfully during the earlier civil rights struggle, had broken down. Issues such as "quotas" and the Middle-East, among others, served to widen the gap which was dividing the two groups. In 1983, when a conference was convened to confront Black-Jewish relations, it was structured around the personalities of Heschel and King. By exploring their lives and teachings, it was hoped that a common spiritual ground might be laid, out of which a constructive dialogue on sensitive issues could grow. The brochure announcing the conference tells us:

> Abraham Joshua Heschel and Martin Luther King were spiritual leaders, whose thoughts, teachings, and deeds inspired Americans of all faiths to join together to work for racial and social justice. . . . An examination of the lives and works of these two brilliant and loving human beings reminds us of how much can be accomplished when we take our religious commitments seriously. Through their spiritual energy, they helped spark a great religious awakening during the late 1950's and 1960's that aroused many of us from our lethargy. . . . Today their vision is needed more than ever. . . . We hope that everyone participating in this Heschel-King conference will leave a little more determined to overcome the differences that divide us and to work together to build the kind of coalition of conscience that will galvanize us once again.[20]

The poor and the humiliated elected Heschel.

The eloquence of his voice and the power of his word were heard again and again on behalf of the neglected and the forlorn. He once said he was propelled out of the security of the ivory tower of research into the swirling domain of public issues because of his study of the prophets. "Prophecy," he wrote, "is the voice that God has lent to the silent agony, a voice to the plundered poor. . . . God is raging in the prophet's words."[21] In Heschel's voice was heard an echo of that rage.

The aged elected Heschel.

He was their most understanding and eloquent spokesman. In 1961 the first White House Conference on Aging found some 6,000 delegates in attendance. Hundreds of sessions took place and countless papers from noted authorities were given. However, one address—Heschel's—overwhelmed the assembly. It was selected as the single representative statement for the conference and it appeared in the congressional record, as well as on the official recording, whose other side contains the address of President Eisenhower. These are the closing words of Heschel's address:

> We must seek ways to overcome the traumatic fear of being old, the prejudice, the discrimination against those advanced in years. All men are created equal, including those advanced in years. Being old is not necessarily the same as being stale. The effort to restore the dignity of old age will depend upon our ability to revive the equation of old age and wisdom. Wisdom is the substance upon which the inner security of the old will forever depend. But the attainment of wisdom is the work of a lifetime.
>
> Old men need a vision, not only recreation.
> Old men need a dream, not only a memory.
> It takes three things to attain a sense of significant being:
> > God
> > A Soul
> > And a Moment
> And the three are always here.
> Just to be is a blessing. Just to live is holy.[22]

Function does not always determine value. Society is not the final arbiter. "God, A Soul, and A Moment . . . are *always* here." Even when we are sick; even when we are alone; even when we are no longer "productive" or "useful"; even when we can no longer hear, or speak, or see. "Just to be," is enough. "Just to live is holy."

The "Six Million" elected Heschel.

His inaugural address at The Union Theological Seminary before a distinguished body of Christian leaders, began thus:

I speak as a member of a congregation whose founder was Abraham, and the name of my Rabbi is Moses. I speak as a person who was able to leave Warsaw, the city in which I was born, just six weeks before the disaster began. My destination was New York, it would have been Auschwitz or Treblinka. I am a brand plucked from the fire, on which my people was burned to death. I am a brand plucked from the fire of an altar of Satan on which millions of human lives were exterminated to evil's greater glory, and on which so much else was consumed: the divine image of so many human beings, many people's faith in the God of justice and compassion, and much of the secret and power of attachment to the Bible bred and cherished in the hearts of men for nearly 2,000 years.[23]

The six million elected him because Heschel composed their epitaph and was their truest witness. He delivered their unforgettable eulogy in his book, *The Earth is the Lord's,* in which he sketched the lasting values of East European Jewry, and which he wrote while still in Cincinnati during the war years. I saw him daily at that time, but rarely did he discuss what must have grieved him most, the end of the thousand-year period of East European Jewry, which he called "The golden era of Jewish history."[24] Instead of describing the horror—the "Holocaust"—he preferred to write about what was most enduring from that golden era—its beauty, its meaning, its holiness. He referred me to a short story, written by a friend of his, in which a Hasidic Master warned his disciples, in the name of sanity, not to dwell overmuch upon the horrors that were to come, citing as proof the Book of Exodus, in which only the first few chapters deal with the sufferings of slavery, while the preponderance of the volume dwells upon the "going out from Egypt."[25] Of course, we need both records—the Holocaust and the Holiness. It was the way of Heschel, however, to choose the affirmative portrayal of the noble. Of East European Jewry, he wrote:

The little Jewish communities in Eastern Europe were like sacred texts opened before the eyes of God, so close were their houses of worship to Mount Sinai. In their humble wooden synagogues, looking as if they were deliberately closing themselves off from the world, the Jews purified the souls that God had given them. . . . They did not write songs. They themselves were songs.[26]

The Russian Jews elected Heschel.

He was among the first to alert us to the calamity in those early years when few were aware of it. (He urged Elie Weisel to travel to Russia, the result of which was his book, *The Jews of Silence*—Jews, that is, who speak out of fear, in silence, with their eyes.) Heschel's plea on behalf of Russian Jews led to rescue efforts that brought thousands of them into freedom. Heschel used to remind us that "the Russian Jews will do more for us than we will ever do for them." He was referring to the courageous example of those who persisted as Jews for 75 years without synagogues, religious schools or books, and against the vicious anti-religious and anti-semitic apparatus of the Soviet Government. In one of his early addresses he compared modern Jewry's attitude toward the Russian Jews to the attitude of ancient Jewry toward the Ten Lost Tribes:

> One of the tragic failures of ancient Judaism was the indifference of our people to the Ten Tribes of Israel which were carried away into exile by Assyria after the Northern Kingdom of Samaria was destroyed. Uncared for, unattended to, overlooked, and abandoned, the ten tribes were consigned to oblivion. . . . At the end they vanished. . . . There is a nightmare that terrifies me today: the unawareness of our being involved in a new failure, in a tragic dereliction of duty.
>
> East European Jewry vanished. Russian Jewry is the last remnant of a people destroyed in extermination camps, the last remnant of a spiritual glory that is no more. . . . Let the twentieth century not enter the annals of Jewish history as the century of physical and spiritual destruction.[27]

The Catholics, the Protestants, the Blacks, among others—all respected Heschel as a *Nasi,* a prince of his people.

Shalem: A Complete Person

Who was Rabbi Abraham Joshua Heschel? He was *shalem,* a complete person, a person marvelously whole.

Consider the worlds of his *environment*.

Born in Warsaw, Poland, in 1907, a descendent of an illustrious line of Hasidic Rabbis, even from early childhood Heschel was viewed with great expectations. At the age of 4 or 5, scholars would place him on a table and interrogate him for the surprising and amusing answers he would give. When his father died during his tenth year, there were those who wanted the young boy to succeed him almost at once. He had already mastered many of the classical religious texts; he had begun to write; and the words he spoke were a strange combination of maturity and youth. The sheer joy he felt as a child, so uncontainable at times that he would burst out in laughter when he met a good friend in the street, was later tamed into an easy sense of humor that added to his special personal charm. But there was also astounding knowledge, keen understanding, and profound feeling: an awareness that human beings dwell on the tangent of the infinite, within the holy dimension; that human life is part of the life of God. Some Hasidic leaders felt that he might bring about a renewal of their movement, which had grown dormant in the twentieth century. Others were aware of the new light that was glowing in their midst. Speaking about his early childhood, Heschel wrote in a rare personal note:

> I was born in Warsaw, Poland, but my cradle stood in Mezbizh (a small town in the province of Podolia, Ukraine), where the Baal Shem Tov, founder of the Hasidic movement, lived during the last twenty years of his life. That is where my father came from, and he continued to regard it as his home. . . .
>
> I was named after my grandfather, Reb Abraham Joshua Heschel—"The Apter Rav," and last great rebbe of Mezbizh. He was marvelous in all his ways, and it was as if the Baal Shem Tov had come to life in him. . . .
>
> Enchanted by a wealth of traditions and tales, I felt truly at home in Mezbizh. That little town so distant from Warsaw and yet so near was the place to which my childish imagination went on many journeys.[28]

It can be said with certainty that the years in Warsaw provided that nourishment of spirit and intellect, that inner dignity and awareness of who he was, which gave permanent direction to Heschel's life. It could not, however, prevent him from peering beyond and, in the end, setting out from his home to explore the world of western civilization which thundered and glittered about him. Departing from Warsaw in his teens, he traveled first to Vilna, where he pursued his secular education and joined a promising group of young Yiddish poets; then on to Berlin, the metropolis of science and philosophy in the 1920s, where he immersed himself in the culture of the West and began to publish his first books and establish his career.

He claimed he was no longer a Hasid. He had indeed abandoned their style of dress and their restricted social contacts for the larger world, both Jewish and German. But somehow Hasidism remained within Heschel:

> In my childhood and in my youth, I was the recipient of many blessings, I lived in the presence of quite a number of extraordinary persons I could revere. And just as I lived as a child in their presence, their presence continues to live in me as an adult. And yet I am not just a dwelling place for other people, an echo of the past. . . . I disagree with those who think of the present in the past tense. . . . The greatest danger is to become obsolete. I try not to be stale. I try to remain young. I have one talent and that is the capacity to be tremendously surprised, surprised at life, at ideas. This is to me the supreme Hasidic imperative.[29]

To the end Heschel remained an anomaly. Most of those who had left the narrow Hasidic milieu of Eastern Europe for the modern, open society of the West—especially if they pursued studies in the humanities—exchanged the one world for the other, often repudiating their Hasidic origins. This was true even of those engaged in Jewish research. The art, philosophy, and literature of the West, as well as its power and apparent freedom, were more than attractive, they were overwhelming. The enthusiastic reviews of Heschel's early works, *Die Prophetie* and *Maimonides,* confirmed how highly he was considered according to the West's own scientific and literary standards. Nonetheless, while mastering European *Kultur* and *Wissenschaft* and recognizing their values, Heschel retained his own religious position and even his Hasidic bias.

In 1952 he gave a memorable description of the conflict he experienced between Berlin and Warsaw, between the intellectual claim of the university and the way of Torah:

> I came with great hunger to the University of Berlin to study philosophy. I looked for a system of thought, for the depth of the spirit, for the meaning of existence. Erudite and profound scholars gave courses in Logic, Epistemology, Esthetics, Ethics and Metaphysics. . . .
>
> Yet, in spite of the intellectual power and honesty which I was priviliged to witness, I became increasingly aware of the gulf that

separated my views from those held at the university. . . . To
them, religion was a feeling. To me, religion included the insights
of the Torah which is a vision of man from the point of view of
God. They spoke of God from the point of view of man. To them
God was an idea, a postulate of reason. They granted Him the
status of being a logical possibility. But to assume that he had
existence would have been a crime against epistemology. . . .

In those months in Berlin I went through moments of profound
bitterness. I felt very much alone with my own problems and
anxieties. I walked alone in the evenings through the magnificent
streets of Berlin. I admired the solidity of its architecture, the
overwhelming drive and power of a dynamic civilization. There
were concerts, theatres, and lectures by famous scholars about the
latest theories and inventions, and I was pondering whether to go
to the new Max Reinhardt play or to a lecture about the theory of
relativity.

Suddenly I noticed the sun had gone down, evening had
arrived. . . .

I had forgotten God. I had forgotten Sinai—I had forgotten
that sunset is my business—that my task is "to restore the world to
the Kingship of the Lord." So I began to utter the words of the
evening prayer.

Blessed Art Thou, Lord Our God,
King Of The Universe
Who By His Word Brings On The Evenings. . . .

On that evening in the streets of Berlin, I was not in a mood to
pray. My heart was heavy, my soul was sad. It was difficult for the
lofty words of prayer to break through the dark clouds of my inner
life.

But how would I dare not to pray? How would I dare to miss
an evening prayer?[30]

Forced to flee the Nazis, Heschel made his way, through Poland
and England, to the United States. After half a decade at The Hebrew
Union College in Cincinnati, the rest of his years here were spent in his
small, crowded study at the Jewish Theological Seminary in New
York from which his works emanated and to which many made
pilgrimage. In Eastern Europe Heschel acquired his ancestral learning
and piety; in Berlin, his philosophy, method, and European culture; in
the United States, within the blessing of a free society which he
treasured, the full extent of his power was reached.

If the worlds of his environment were universal, so were the worlds
of his *scholarship*. What he wrote of Maimonides—that "his

achievement seems so incredible that one is almost inclined to believe
that Maimonides is the name for a whole academy of scholars rather
than the name of an individual"[31]—could be said of Heschel himself.
He contributed major works in fields each of which required their own
separate disciplines: Bible, rabbinics, philosophy, Hasidism, theology,
and ethics, among others. It was this mastery of virtually the entire
range of Jewish creative experience, as well as that of Western culture,
which contributed to the richness of his thinking. He was equally
gifted in four languages—Yiddish, Hebrew, German, and English—
and would select the language of the book he was engaged in
according to its subject.

Such scholarship had two requirements, at least: a lucid mind and
a determined will. Heschel possessed both. He accepted the old Jewish
view that "Living is not a private affair of the individual. Living is
what man does with God's time, what man does with God's world."[32]
"Life is . . . a task, not a game, a command, not a favor."[33] For the
scholar this means never to waste precious hours or energy. Petty
controversy, for example, was to be avoided at all costs. Once, after an
unpleasant confrontation, he told me a story about his uncle, a famed
hasidic rabbi. During a nasty dispute between his own hasidic sect and
another, he kept silent to his friends' appeal for support. When asked
why, he quoted the Talmud: "The fence around wisdom is silence."
"But," he added, "silence is only the fence; what is the wisdom? That
petty controversy does not even concern me!" Heschel admonished
me not to forget the tale.

Heschel's immense productivity, despite being uprooted twice
from his cultural milieu, was not unrelated to his understanding that,
with the ending of East European Jewry, he was one of the few who
could leave the record of what had been. He felt a solemn burden: to
pass this legacy on to the next generation. How then could one waste
valuable time?

> A world has vanished. All that remains is a sanctuary hidden in the
> realm of the spirit. We of this generation are still holding the key.
> Unless we remember, unless we unlock it, the treasury of the ages
> will remain a secret of God. . . . We are either the last Jews or
> those who will hand over the entire past to generations to come.[34]

Heschel, above all, held that key. And he lived with the knowledge
that he held it.

Finally, in addition to the worlds of his environment and his
scholarship, the worlds of Heschel's *concern* were likewise universal,

bridging the divisions which tend to divide Jews, to divide persons, and to divide religions. His effort in this latter respect was notable.

Heschel reached out a hand to those of other faiths because of the depth, not the shallowness, of his own spiritual life: the deeper the roots, the broader the branches. Or, as one Christian scholar noted, "Heschel was most human as he was most Jewish."[35] His ecumenical call was grounded in his belief that human life partakes in the life of God; that human beings dwell both in the realm of nature and the dimension of the holy. The divine image, and not only the chromosome and the circulatory system, is the common bond of humankind. Beneath the divisiveness of creeds lie those underpinnings of religion, such as humility, compassion, awe, and faith, which characterize the community of all true persons of spirit. "Different are the languages of prayer," he wrote, "but the tears are the same."[36] If divine unity means that God is not only "one in Himself" but striving to be one with humanity, as Heschel believed, then the goal of God requires the work of human beings. Animosity impedes; fellowship advances the reign of Heaven. It was this spiritual fraternity of humankind which Heschel acted upon in his ecumenical relations. His effort to nurture this bond was responded to so warmly by others, because their spirits, not only their minds, were touched.

He did so, as well, because he knew that if the divine fellowship did not enjoin us, a demonic one would. For humanness is not static, and we are "either the ministers of the sacred, or slaves of evil."[37] While some are "wary of the ecumenical movement," he wrote, "there is another ecumenical movement, worldwide in influence: nihilism. We must choose between interfaith and inter-nihilism."[38]

> *No religion is an island.* We are all involved with one another. Spiritual betrayal on the part of one of us affects the faith of all of us. Views adopted in one community have an impact on other communities. Today religious isolationism is a myth. . . . Should we refuse to be on speaking terms with one another and hope for each other's failure? Or should we pray for each other's health, and help one another in preserving one's respective legacy, in preserving a common legacy.[39]

An example of how Heschel was perceived by gentiles comes from the letter of an executive of the Bell System. He told how in the 1960s this corporation had an arrangement with Dartmouth College whereby each summer 15 of its more promising members of middle management spent 8 weeks in Hanover, New Hampshire, studying the

Humanities and meeting special guests invited for a 24-hour period. In the summer of 1964, Heschel was such a guest. Despite the passage of a decade-and-a-half, Heschel's theme—the dignity, uniqueness, and sacredness of being human—was still fresh in mind. Of his encounter with Heschel, the executive wrote:

> You must understand that the Bell System group was made up of middle-aged, gentile business executives, whose normal concerns were those of the corporation, and yet each member of the group was, I remember, struck by the aura of reverence, wisdom, and concern for mankind which seemed to emanate from Rabbi Heschel. In my own case, I felt that his thoughts were communicated to me through a medium far beyond his words. If, when he had finished, he had risen and beckoned me to follow, I would have done so without questions. Even after 15 years, I am convinced that, on that day, I sat with a Biblical prophet.[40]

Heschel's environment, his scholarship, and his concern were each characterized by an unusually broad range. This contributed to the wholeness of his person: the breadth of his understanding, as well as its depth.

Zaddik of the Generation

We have said that Heschel was a *Nasi,* a prince of his people, and *Shalem,* a whole person. Let us pose the question a final time. Who was Heschel?

He was a *zaddik,* the zaddik of his generation.

Behind his public face as thinker, writer, and advocate, was a private undisclosed frame—the zaddik, the hasidic master, that remarkable new leader who emerged from the movement of Hasidism, and who renewed the life of eighteenth and nineteenth-century East-European Jewry. Martin Buber believed that "the Zaddikim . . . offer us a number of religious personalities of a vitality, a spiritual strength, a manifold originality such as never, to my knowledge, appeared together in so short a timespan in the history of religion."[41] Heschel must be understood, in good measure, against the pattern of those masters. Since succession in Hasidic leadership was dynastic, Heschel, as a member of that royalty, had been raised to sit upon the zaddik's throne, as his father and his father's father had done before. Indeed, of him even more was expected. And yet, though he abdicated his destined role by departing for the west, that is what he ultimately became: a zaddik—the zaddik of his generation.[42]

The zaddik was both scholar and pietist, master of prayer and teacher of Torah, bound up with God and the center of the community, wielder of power yet humble, a teacher by example as well as by word, one who affirmed life by celebrating it in joy, whose every act was meant to glorify God. When we consider Heschel's life and work against this description, we see how he approximated it.

The zaddik was bound up with God. The Hasidic admonition was to do as the Psalmist said: "I have set the Lord before me at all times." At *all* times. Heschel once remarked to me: "One can only speak of God in the presence of God." What a guideline for theologians!

Heschel's rich inner life was sustained primarily by prayer, about which he has given us as profound an analysis as we possess. That analysis—descriptive, analytical, poetic, suggestive—is surely, in part, personal.

> Prayer is spiritual ecstasy. It is as if all our vital thoughts in fierce ardor would burst the mind to stream toward God. A keen single force draws our yearning for the utmost out of the seclusion of the soul. We try to see our visions in His light, to feel our life as His affair. We begin by letting the thought of Him engage our minds, by realizing His name and entering into a reverie which leads through beauty and stillness, from feeling to thought, and from understanding to devotion.[43]

In the mid-forties, Heschel initiated me into the regimen of daily worship. I would join him in his room at dawn to pray the morning service. Those were unforgettable hours. With his large prayer shawl about him and his phylacteries on his head and arm, he paced the room reciting the long pages by heart, at first slowly and softly but then more quickly and loudly, the words flowing as a torrent from him, at times roaring like a lion, rising at last to a culmination of motionless silence, all within. Time opened to eternity.

Beyond the word was the song, especially the song without words, the *nigun,* the preferred hasidic musical form. Once at a gathering at Heschel's home, he was asked to sing the words of his favorite Yiddish song, to which he replied with a laugh that his favorite Yiddish song had no words. Those melodies of yearning and ecstasy which he would sing at twilight at the close of the sabbath melted the heart, so that in the anonymity of growing darkness, one felt only the bond of spirit.

The task of the zaddik was to seek out the sparks of holiness everywhere, even amidst evil. This too was characteristic of Heschel. He often restrained himself from unnecessary criticism, even when under attack, preferring to dwell upon the virtues of others. This was characteristic of his positive approach to life: How sad, I once observed, that a forthcoming wedding consisted of two orphans who would be bereft of family at the festivities. How wonderful, Heschel corrected me, that two orphans, each with no one else, had found each other! After a luncheon together one day, I remarked on the good meal. "Better not to comment on the quality of food," he said. "Let the blessing suffice. For if today the meal is good, tomorrow it may be bad, and how can you say that the food God gives us for life is bad?"

Isolation was anathema to the zaddik. Indeed, to the classic hasidic writers Noah was decried as the symbol of the unconcerned leader, because he "walked *with* God," that is, in such selfish seclusion that he caused the flood; while Abraham was acclaimed as the symbol of the zaddik, because he walked *"before"* God "in the midst of the city," and would have prevented the deluge had he lived earlier.[44] So it was with Heschel. His door was open to all. And they came, not only with problems of the intellect, but with problems of life. Other scholars protected their privacy and were unavailable. Not so Heschel.

The zaddik stood for exalted leadership, believing that all could be changed by a true master. Decrying the mediocrity of those wielding power today, Heschel once observed to me that this was an old problem. While scripture says, "Moses chose able men to become rulers over the people" (Exodus, 18:25), only a few verses before we are told that in addition to "able men" he was looking for "men who feared God, men of truth, who hated unjust gain" (vs. 20). Why did Moses settle for those possessing only one out of four qualities? Alas, sighed Heschel, even Moses had problems finding competent leaders! In class each year Heschel would recall the answer that the German poet, Rainer Maria Rilke, gave to the young man who wrote, asking whether he should become a poet: Only if you cannot live without being a poet! That was Heschel's advice to incipient rabbis (or priests): become a rabbi only if your life depends upon it. Before his death, Moses prayed for a worthy successor—"Let the Lord set a man over the congregation, who will go out before them and will come in before them . . . that the congregation of the Lord be not as sheep which have no shepherd" (Num. 27:18). Heschel would quote the interpretation of a Hasidic master: To "go out before them" can be translated in Yiddish as *"ois-gehen far zé,"* which means, one who is willing to die for them!

For the zaddik, the task of creating a righteous people was a divine command.. Hasidic society, which was marked by a community of Hasidim around their particular zaddik, strove to achieve a fellowship of love, responsibility, and justice. It represented, in microcosm, a model pattern of community. The struggle for righteousness includes a concomitant struggle against evil; to despair, or to withdraw from that ongoing effort, is tantamount to denial. Heschel was discouraged by the failure of European theologians to adequately contend with the oncoming horror of Nazism, a failure which he ascribed, in part, to the prevailing belief in human worthlessness and helplessness. He told me how, shortly before the war, in 1938, he visited Switzerland, and was impressed with the work of Ragatz, a theologian who, with a number of followers, had turned against theology, was deep into the Hebrew Bible, and was devoting himself to social institutions and politics in the belief that the only hope at that moment was to come to the aid of fellow human beings. He also went to Basel, then under the influence of Karl Barth. "When I asserted that in this time of the rise of totalitarianism the single most important task for religious persons is to understand and work for a just state," Heschel said, "I was met with rejection. Even accused of being an atheist. After all, I did not talk theology. What could one expect of man, they argued, was he not depraved and beyond the hope of history?"

The zaddik not only taught Torah, he was Torah, a living Torah. His disciples learned from his life, not only his words. On the anniversary of the death of Albert Schweitzer, Heschel would recount the latter's life in class: How he forsook glory as a famed philosopher, organist, and musicologist, to become a common doctor in a clinic in deepest Africa as atonement for the sins of the white race. In the last chapter of his book on Maimonides, Heschel proposed a solution to a paradox that has long puzzled scholars. Toward the end of his life, Maimonides, a giant in philosophy, law, and science, advised his translator, Ibn Tibbon, by letter, not to take the long journey from Europe to visit him in Egypt, because he could spend little time with him even were he to come. There follows an exhausting itinerary of Maimonides' schedule of daily medical work from early dawn to late evening with time only for a single meal. Why? Why did he forsake his momentous unfinished scholarly works to heal the sick, which any doctor could have done? Heschel suggests an answer:

This is Maimonides' last metamorphosis: From metaphysics to medicine, from contemplation to practice, from speculation to the imitation of God. . . . Preoccupation with the concrete man and

the effort to aid him in his suffering is now the form of religious
devotion. . . . Personal achievement is abandoned for enhancing
God's presence in human deeds.[45]

What Heschel said of Maimonides, could be said of himself. Despite
the frailty of his health, the preciousness of each hour of his life, the
books yet to be written that were laid out so clearly in his mind, he
spent more and more time in the last years of his life on the social
issues: civil rights, the Vietnam war, the plight of Russian Jewry, etc.
Prayer had become deed.

The zaddik was the master of communication. Profound in his
learning, yet he knew how to reach the people. Hasidism succeeded,
Heschel said, because while it developed a subtle, sophisticated
mysticism for the elite, it also knew how to bring the living God to the
people. This too was a characteristic of Heschel. On the one hand he
was all scholar and philosopher; on the other, the flash of humor, the
illuminating story, the apt phrase, the genius for summing up.

With the appearance of his now widely celebrated first book, *The
Earth is the Lord's,* which portrayed the lowly East European Jew in a
most favorable light, Heschel became the frequent butt of criticism. At
one social gathering, a well-known guest turned to him and said:

> In the town in Poland that I came from, I knew an old Hasid. He
> would rise at the outlandish hour of five o'clock in the morning,
> make his way to the synagogue, where he would proceed to disturb
> everyone with his loud, endless prayers and his study, never
> pausing for breakfast or lunch, until about five o'clock in the
> afternoon when he took some nourishment. Now tell me, is that
> what you call religion? Is that a sensible life for a man?

Though pained, Heschel appeared to be listening thoughtfully. He
replied:

> Isn't that strange. I know someone just like that right here in New
> York. He is almost an exact parallel to that old Hasid. He, too,
> gets up very early in the morning, devotes himself with single-
> minded passion to his work, and hardly tastes food during the day
> until late in the afternoon. Indeed, he worked so hard that at
> forty-two he suffered a stroke! There is only one difference
> between the two—the purpose of this one's work is Gold! Now, tell
> me, is such behavior commensurate with reason or common sense?
> Yet, you belittle the one and probably admire the other. Why?

"But that Hasid didn't *do* anything with his life," answered the guest. "Who cared about his prayer and study?"

"Isn't it possible," Heschel quietly responded, "that God cared?"

According to his own testimony, two opposite Hasidic masters served as models to Heschel: the Baal Shem Tov, the founder of Hasidism, and his counterpart, Rabbi Mendl of Kotzk. About their influence on him, he wrote:

> The earliest fascination I can recall is associated with the Baal Shem, whose parables disclosed some of the first insights I gained as a child. He remained a model too sublime to follow, yet too overwhelming to ignore.
>
> It was in my ninth year that the presence of Reb Menahem Mendl of Kotzk, known as the Kotzker, entered my life. Since then he has remained a steady companion and a haunting challenge. Although he often stunted me, he also urged me to confront perplexities that I might have preferred to evade.
>
> Years later I realized that, in being guided by both the Baal Shem Tov and the Kotzker, I had allowed two forces to carry on a struggle within me. . . . The one reminded me that there could be a Heaven on earth, the other shocked me into discovering Hell in the alleged Heavenly places in our world. . . . The Baal Shem dwelled in my life like a lamp, while the Kotzker struck like lightning.[46]

As in his philosophy, so in his life, a polarity of ways prevailed: the love, forgiveness, beauty, and gentleness of the Baal Shem; and the contempt for fraud, the fearless pursuit of truth of the Kotzker.

As a master in the tradition of the Kotzk, Heschel spoke out boldly. His words were felt as a hammer upon a rock. Sparks lit up the darkness of apathy.

"Religion has declined," he told religious leaders, "not because it was refuted, but because it became irrelevent, dull, oppressive, insipid. . . . When religion speaks only in the name of authority rather than with the voice of compassion, its message becomes meaningless."[47] "One is embarrassed to be called religious," he told one audience, "in the face of religion's failures to keep alive the image of God in the face of man. . . . We have imprisoned God in our sanctuaries and slogans, and now the word of God is dying on our lips."[48] He warned theologians that "a theory of God can easily become a substitute for God, impressive to the mind when God as a living reality is absent from the soul."[49] Heschel chided Reform rabbis for their prejudice against the Law: "Let us beware lest we reduce the Bible to literature, Jewish observance to good manners, the Talmud to Emily Post."[50] He admonished Orthodox Jewish leaders for an "all or nothing" approach to the Law: "The intransigent refuse to surrender a single iota, yet are ready to surrender the multitudes of Israel."[51] To Conservative rabbis he complained of synagogue services without life: "Our motto is monotony. The fire has gone out of our worship. It is cold, stiff, and dead."[52] Before an assembly of religious educators, he insisted that *"the vapidity and trivialization of religious instruction"*[53] is the major reason why attendance at religious schools has generally failed to shape the character and attitudes of our children. While reminding doctors at an American Medical Association convention that "Medicine is a sacred art," he spoke also of "the nightmare of medical bills," of "the private hospitals that refuse to admit a human being in agony unless cash is offered in advance," and of how "making money may cost us values that no money can buy."[54] (The San Francisco paper the following day ran a headline: "Dr. Heschel's Bitter Pill"!) To all of us Heschel cried out: "The taste for the good has all but gone from the earth. . . . The horrors of our time fill our souls with reproach and everlasting shame."[55]

Few were to depart from such lectures unchanged. The words were in the spirit of the Master of Kotzk.

But even more than a cry for justice, one heard from Heschel a call to grandeur, to compassion, to hope, a song of celebration and exhaltation. It was the voice of the other, still greater, master: the Baal Shem Tov.

Heschel reminded his audiences and readers that although human guilt seems endless, "there is always a way that leads out of guilt: repentance or turning to God," that "over all the darkness of experience hovers the vision of a different day."[56] He reminded us that although "the vision of the sacred has all but died in the soul of man,"[57] still human beings can be "a fulfillment of the vision of God."[58] "To pray is to dream in league with God, to envision His holy visions."[59] "God's dream is not to be alone," said Heschel, but "to have mankind as a partner in the drama of continuous creation."[60] Directing a special message to young people shortly before he died, Heschel said:

Remember that there is a meaning beyond absurdity, . . . that every little deed counts, that every word has power, and that we can all do our share to redeem the world. . . . And above all, remember that the meaning of life is to build a life as if it were a work of art.[61]

Finally Heschel told us that although "this is an age of spiritual
blackout, . . . the darkness is neither final nor complete. . . . We are
called . . . to defy absurdity and despair and to wait for God to say
again: Let there be light. And there will be light."[62]

How could one hear such words and not listen to their echo, and
re-echo, not recall them again and again, not ponder them, and be
changed by them?

Who was Rabbi Abraham Joshua Heschel? He was *nasi,* a prince
of his people. He was *shalem,* marvelously whole. He was *zaddik
hador,* a master for our age.

The light of Heschel draws from flames first kindled long ago upon
altars high and holy where prophets and priests, sages and masters
served: where mind and heart and deed were one. During these days of
fellowship in his memory, let us strive to become aware of the
common spirit which binds us together as children of the single God.

Notes

1. Susannah Heschel, in an address at a conference on A. J. Heschel
   sponsored by the Chicago Board of Jewish Education, February 20–21,
   1983.
2. Rabbi Alter Yisrael Perlow (1874–1933); cf. S. H. Dresner, "The
   Contribution of Abraham Joshua Heschel," *Judaism,* 32 (Winter 1982),
   57–69, pp. 62–63.
3. Abraham Joshua Heschel, *Man Is Not Alone: A Philosophy of Religion*
   (New York: Farrar, Straus, and Young, 1951), p. 282; hereafter cited as
   Not Alone.
4. Cf. "Editorial: Contemporary Judaism and the Christian," *America,* 128
   (March 10, 1973), p. 202.
5. John C. Merkle, *The Genesis of Faith: The Depth Theology of Abraham
   Joshua Heschel* (New York: Macmillan Publishing Co., 1985).
6. Some of my remarks are in the first person; I knew Heschel intimately
   from 1942, two years after his arrival in America, and much is drawn
   from a diary of conversations with him which I kept from 1949 to 1953.
7. Personal communication, S. Noble.
8. Reinhold Niebuhr, "Masterly Analysis of Faith," *New York Herald
   Tribune Book Review,* 118 (April 1, 1951), p. 12.
9. Martin Marty, *The Christian Century,* 19 (January 17, 1973), p. 87.
10. E. A. Bayne, pamphlet published by the Center for Mediterranean
    Studies in Rome, 1973.
11. Letter from E. A. Bayne to Samuel H. Dresner, December 29, 1982.
12. *Ibid.*
13. Bayne, pamphlet, *op. cit.*
14. *Ibid.*
15. *Ibid.*

16. Bayne, correspondence, *op. cit.*
17. Abraham Joshua Heschel, quoted in *Conservative Judaism*, 22 (Spring 1968), p. 1.
18. Martin Luther King, quoted in *Ibid.*, pp. 1–2.
19. Abraham Joshua Heschel, *The Insecurity of Freedom: Essays on Human Existence* (New York: Schocken Books, 1966), p. 85; hereafter cited as *Freedom.*
20. The Heschel–King Conference, sponsored by the Indiana Interreligious commission on Human Equality, took place on November 11, 1983 in Indianapolis, IN.
21. Abraham Joshua Heschel, *The Prophets* (New York: Harper and Row, 1962), p. 5.
22. *Freedom*, p. 84.
23. Abraham Joshua Heschel, "No Religion Is An Island," *Union Seminary Quarterly Review*, 21 (January 1966), 117–134, p. 117.
24. Abraham Joshua Heschel, *The Earth Is the Lord's: The Inner World of the Jew In Eastern Europe* (New York: Henry Schuman, Inc., 1950), p. 10; hereafter cited as *Earth.*
25. Cf. Fischel Schneirson, *"Ani Maamin"* ("I Believe"); English translation by S. Dresner, *Conservative Judaism*, 22 (Spring 1968), 20–30.
26. *Earth*, pp. 92–93.
27. *Freedom*, pp. 271, 273.
28. Abraham Joshua Heschel, *A Passion for Truth* (New York: Farrar, Straus, and Giroux, 1973), p. xiii; hereafter cited as *Truth.*
29. Abraham Joshua Heschel, "In Search of Exaltation," *Jewish Heritage*, 13 (Fall 1971), 29–30, 35, p. 29.
30. Abraham Joshua Heschel, *Man's Quest for God: Studies in Prayer and Symbolism* (New York: Charles Scribner's Sons, 1954), pp. 94–98; hereafter cited as *Quest.*
31. *Freedom*, p. 285.
32. Abraham Joshua Heschel, *God In Search of Man: A Philosophy of Judaism* (New York: Farrar, Straus, and Cudahy, 1955), p. 356; hereafter cited as *Search.*
33. *Not Alone*, p. 294.
34. *Earth*, p. 107.
35. W. D. Davies, "Conscience, Scholar, Witness," *America*, 128 (March 10, 1973), 213–215, p. 215.
36. *Freedom*, p. 180.
37. *Earth*, p. 107.
38. "No Religion Is an Island," p. 119.
39. *Ibid.*
40. Letter from S. H. Washburn to Samuel H. Dresner, March 20, 1979.
41. Martin Buber, *Hasidism* (New York: Philosophical Library, 1945), pp. 3–4.
42. Cf. Samuel H. Dresner, *The Zaddik* (New York: Abelard-Schuman, 1960; Schocken, 1974).
43. *Quest*, pp. 18–19.
44. Cf. *The Zaddik, op. cit.,* chapters 4 and 7.

45. *Freedom,* p. 290.

46. *Truth,* pp. xiv–xv.

47. *Freedom,* pp. 3–4; from an address entitled "Religion in a Free Society" delivered in 1958 at a seminar on Religion in a Free Society, sponsored by the Fund for the Republic.

48. *Freedom,* p. 165; from an address entitled "Sacred Image of Man," delivered in 1957 at the annual convention of the Religious Education Association, in Chicago, IL.

49. Abraham Joshua Heschel, "The Jewish Notion of God and Christian Renewal," *Renewal of Religious Thought,* Vol. I of *Theology of Renewal,* ed. by L. K. Shook (New York: Herder & Herder, 1968), 105–129, p. 106; from an address to a congress of Catholic Theologians in Toronto, 1967.

50. *Quest,* p. 113; from an address originally entitled "Toward an Understanding of Halacha" delivered in 1953 at the annual convention of the Central Conference of American Rabbis, in Estes Park, CO.

51. *Freedom,* p. 205; from an address entitled "The Individual Jew and His Obligations" delivered in 1957 at the Jerusalem Ideological Conference, convened at Hebrew University in Jerusalem.

52. *Quest,* p. 149; from an address originally entitled "The Spirit of Prayer" delivered in 1953 at the annual convention of The Rabbinical Assembly of America, in Atlantic City, NJ.

53. *Freedom,* p. 53; from an address entitled "Idols In the Temple," delivered in 1962 at the annual convention of the Religious Education Association, in Chicago, IL.

54. *Ibid.,* pp. 33, 35, 34; from an address entitled "The Patient as a Person" delivered in 1964 at the annual convention of the American Medical Association, in San Francisco, CA.

55. *Quest,* p. 148; from an address in 1938 to an assembly of Quakers in Berlin; expanded into an article published in a 1943 issue of *The Hebrew Union College Bulletin.*

56. *Freedom,* p. 165.

57. *Quest,* p. 149.

58. *Not Alone,* p. 205.

59. *Quest,* p. 19.

60. Abraham Joshua Heschel, *Who Is Man?* (Stanford, CA: Stanford University Press, 1965), p. 119.

61. "A Conversation with Dr. Abraham Joshua Heschel," transcript of "The Eternal Light" program, presented February 4, 1973, by the National Broadcasting Company, p. 21. Heschel was interviewed by Carl Stern, NBC News United States Supreme Court Correspondent.

62. Abraham Joshua Heschel, "On Prayer," *Conservative Judaism,* 25 (Fall 1970), 3–12, p. 12.

2

A Tribute to Rabbi Heschel
Banquet Address

WOLFE KELMAN

In the course of my relationship and great priviledge of friendship with Rabbi Heschel, I had the honor of doing many things, some of which were difficult, some easy. What I have to do tonight is indeed difficult, to try to contract a tribute to this great man in the few moments that remain before the concert that is to follow.

It is very appropriate to pay tribute to Rabbi Heschel in the context of a banquet. While sharing this supper, I was thinking of how much Heschel would have appreciated the fact that this commemoration is being celebrated at a *seudah,* at a meal with wine and other spirits. Perhaps you remembered to drink *l'chaim* to his memory. I, at least, under my breath said *zechuto yagen aleinu,* as was done when people gathered to remember a pious and saintly teacher and leader. And I do indeed feel his *zechut,* his merits, his influence, literally hovering over us, protecting and enlarging us this evening.

But I don't want you to think that I'm going to be solemn, because no, Rabbi Heschel was not a solemn man. Shortly after he died I was asked by a reporter what we talked about all the hours that we spent together. I told him that most of the time we laughed. At least I did; I wasn't as funny as he was. Often I remember him in the spirit of laughter—and stories. I can't help but begin with one of those stories that actually happened about 13 years ago or so. Heschel was asked to be the main speaker at a banquet like this, except that it was at the Waldorf Astoria Hotel in New York. The guest of honor was Mordacai Kaplan, who was not exactly an ideological follower of Heschel. But Dr. Heschel, being gracious, accepted the invitation. While enroute to the dinner, he was wondering how he would begin his tribute to Professor Kaplan. And I told him it is customary at American banquets for after-dinner speakers to be witty. "Ah," he said "that's wonderful." So he began his after-dinner address in the following way: "You know, there's nothing that happens in this world that is not first recorded or anticipated in the Bible. So how do we know about after-dinner speeches from the Bible?" He answered his own question by recalling that, in the book of Genesis, when the angels came to visit Abraham (the first Abraham) he was very hospitable and offered them a banquet. Then there was a speech that one of the angels gave. It was one sentence long: "I will visit you again next year and your wife, Sarah, will then have a son." That was the totality of the speech recorded, said Heschel, who then reminded his audience of how Sarah laughed upon overhearing what the angel said. "From this we learn three things," said Heschel: "One, that an after-dinner speech must be brief; two, that it must be witty, as it is written, 'and Sarah laughed'; and three, that it must be pregnant with meaning!"

Well, I'll try to be brief. And witty? No guarantees for that; that's one of those things in the hands of heaven. And I hope I have something to say that has some meaning.

There are so many things I would like to share with you. For example, how much he loved his wife and daughter. I know, and I'm sure they know too, how much time he spent worrying about their comfort, their welfare, various events in their lives and life-cycles. I would like also to tell you a little bit about some of the events that I witnessed and lived through with him. But perhaps at another time when we are together again I'll be able to do that.

I wish to begin, not by being witty, but by sharing with you my sense of awe, literal awe, that we are all here together, sharing this event. It's really an amazing fact, and I don't take it for granted, not at all. If, 20 or 30 years ago, someone had said that we, of different faiths, could gather in this way, perhaps an optimist like Rabbi

Heschel might have believed it, but most of us wouldn't have. And the fact that it's happening is, to me, a source of awe and gratitude, because awe must be followed by gratitude. And I want to acknowledge this gratitude to all who have made this gathering possible. To think that here, in the heart of Minnesota, in the midst of these beautiful surroundings, hundreds of us from different religious faiths have assembled to pay tribute to an immigrant Jew! Yet it does make sense. For the person we honor built many of the bridges that span the oceans which for centuries had separated us. How the waves in those oceans have often overwhelmed us, and drowned us! Awe-inspiring as it is, it seems so appropriate, so natural, to be here together, honoring the person who taught so many of us how to be open to those of other faiths, while retaining our own commitments. It's not easy to be open. It's much easier to be closed, because when we open up we become vulnerable. Opening up to each other, with all its vulnerability, can only happen as an act of love, with a readiness to take risks. It is much easier, and it takes less time and no risk at all, to condemn and to hate those who are different, and to engage in polemics against them. It is this opening to each other that I celebrate and for which I express my gratitude.

I recall Heschel and I talking on several occasions about a very important idea in Judaism, the idea of the *hasidei umoth haolam,* the righteous of all nations. In the Jewish tradition they are considered equal in the eyes of God and in the rewards that await them. Heschel eagerly sought them out, to embrace them, to welcome them. Recently, at a Holocaust gathering in Dallas, Texas, I heard Rabbi Morris Shapiro, who was a disciple of Rabbi Heschel, recalling what Heschel taught him about this doctrine of the *hasidei umoth haolam.* As a disciple should do, Rabbi Shapiro added to his master's teaching. He reminded us that it's easy for those who have been oppressed and persecuted to remember those that did the persecuting, and that it's difficult to remember those who took great risks towards openness. This is because when we remember them and acknowledge them we must ask ourselves what we have done that's equally risky, equally dangerous, equally open. So most of us prefer not to think about those who are righteous and who take great risks. This rabbi reminded us that the tradition of acknowledging the merits of the righteous goes back all the way to the daughter of Pharaoh. She stretched out her hand to rescue one of the first Jews ever left abandoned. And what does the Torah call her? Batya—the daughter of God. She, the daughter of Pharaoh, was called the daughter of God. Why? Because she reached out to rescue a helpless child. It was people like that whom Heschel respected—whom he sought out and cultivated.

Heschel took great pride in being the descendent of the *Ohev Yisroel,* the "lover of Israel," Rabbi Abraham Joshua Heschel of Apt who died in 1825. In fact, as you can see, he was named after him. The real name of the man we honor tonight was Abraham Joshua Heschel Heschel. Right, Sylvia? Most people don't know that he was a double Heschel. His "Christian" name was Abraham Joshua Heschel, and his given name was Heschel. After the Rabbi of Apt died, there were only two words placed on his gravestone: *Ohev Yisroel,* Lover of Israel. Our own Heschel also deeply loved the Jewish people. His was a consuming love, an unconditional love, a love without barriers, transcending denominations. And Heschel had a quality that's rare in all groups; he was able to transcend the love of his own, to embrace those who were other than he, to love them and yet retain his separate otherness. He was open to them without becoming a syncretist, without denying his authenticity, without wavering from meticulous observance and love of his own tradition. While deeply rooted in that tradition, loving it with a consuming passion, he reached out and loved those who were different. This was one of Heschel's great virtues, one of the great lessons he taught us.

He had many special gifts. Of course he had this great *yichus,* great ancestry, which he cherished without being arrogant about it. He also was blessed, by God's grace, with exceptional intellectual qualities, especially a creative imagination. He also did what very few people manage to do and survive intact: to live and absorb four cultures. He mastered each into which he moved, not abandoning the one that he had left, but taking it with him and integrating it. There was the culture of Eastern European Jewry, of which he was a supreme master and translator and teacher. More than any other Jewish theologian of the twentieth century, he was deeply learned Jewishly, not only philosophically and theologically. In addition to his deep roots and authentic Hasidic learning, he also was a master of Yiddish poetry. Yet he was able to take this Eastern European culture to Germany and, in a very short time, master Western learning and Western culture. In such a short period of time, he was writing in German with great skill and effectiveness. He also absorbed contemporary Hebrew culture. He spoke and wrote Hebrew masterfully, beautifully. Finally, we all know of his mastery of the English language, his unparalleled poetic prose. He managed to master and to integrate all of these languages and the cultures they represent.

In addition to this, he had the gift of what I would call perfect spiritual pitch. You know how some people have perfect musical pitch? Heschel was the only person I have ever known who had perfect spiritual pitch. Whenever he spoke, whenever he wrote, whatever the setting, whatever the audience; whether it was with hasidim in a *shtibl* on 101st Street, or in the grandeur of the Vatican, or marching in Selma, wherever it was, it was never off-key. It sounded right, spiritually right, religiously elevating, and never, never false—because, above all, he was a very authentic person. In last week's portion of the Torah we read, amongst the other commandments, *lo sonu ish amisoi,* a man should not defraud his neighbor. Heschel often quoted the Kotzker Rebbe who said that "every Hasid must go beyond the law." But how does one observe beyond the commandment not to deceive a neighbor? The Kotzker's reply *"nisht sich opnaren"*—not to deceive yourself. Heschel certainly never deceived himself. On the contrary, if anything, he tended to underestimate himself, in not knowing how exceedingly wonderful and talented and unusual he was.

Above all, Heschel had passion, *hitahavut.* It was no accident that the title of his last book was *A Passion for Truth.* Throughout his writing one senses this passion in his words. And to be in his presence was to experience a passionate zest for every moment. It was impossible to be bored in his presence, nor do I recall him ever being bored or having to kill time. The very notion of killing time would have been blasphemous to him. He had the capacity to sense the excitement of every moment and to become absorbed in it. I recall joking with him about how some people are like windmills who flail about all the time and how other people are like laserbeams. Both types probably use the same amount of energy, but the energy of the former gets scattered, while the energy of the latter is channeled. Heschel had the capacity for total concentration, like a laserbeam. He was fully alive to each new moment and always retained the sense of wonder and amazement about which he wrote and spoke so convincingly.

Heschel was also a man of great compassion, especially for the poor and the persecuted. And, what is more difficult to achieve, he had compassion and forgiveness for those who had hurt him personally. Yet, because of his perfect spiritual pitch that I spoke about, Rabbi Heschel knew that to forgive harm done to him was quite different than extending forgiveness to those who hurt others. Once when asked if he could forgive the Nazis for their crime against the Jews and others, Heschel responded with the following story.

Many years ago, Reb Chaim, the rabbi of Brisk, a learned man, revered also for his gentleness, boarded a train in Warsaw to return to his home town. A man of slight stature and no apparent distinction, Reb Chaim made his way to a compartment. As he sat there, he was surrounded by traveling salesmen who were enjoying some brandy and a game of cards. As the game progressed and the excitement increased, the rabbi remained aloof, absorbed in prayer and in a book he was reading. Such aloofness annoyed the salesmen who badgered the rabbi to join them at cards. Reb Chaim told them that he never played cards, and he returned to his book. As time passed, the rabbi's aloofness annoyed them even more. One of those present accosted him, saying: "If we're not good enough to play with, we're not good enough to sit with." He then grabbed Reb Chaim and shoved him out of the compartment. For several hours the rabbi had to stand until he reached Brisk.

Brisk was also the destination of the salesmen. When the rabbi left the train he was immediately surrounded by admirers welcoming him home. When the salesmen saw how he was greeted by the crowd they wondered "Who is this man?" When someone told them that he was the famous rabbi of Brisk they were overcome with shame. They immediately went over to Reb Chaim to beg his forgiveness. "I can't forgive you," replied the rabbi. Distraught, the salesmen made their way to the hotel where they would spend the night. But there they found no rest and decided to once again ask the rabbi's forgiveness. They went to his home and there met Reb Chaim. "We'll do any penance you ask, give to any charity you choose, if only you will forgive us." Reb Chaim's answer was brief: "No."

That night the salesmen could not sleep. So, early in the morning, they went to the synagogue to once more implore the rabbi's forgiveness. There they were introduced to the rabbi's son with whom they shared their story. The son could not understand his father's obstinancy and, seeing the anxiety of the men, promised to discuss the matter with his father.

"Father, is it not a Jewish law that we must forgive those who offend us and ask our forgiveness?" "Yes," replied Reb Chaim. "Then Father, *Tate,* why have you not forgiven the salesmen who begged it of you yesterday?" "Velvel"—his name was Velvel the Brisker—"Velvel, you don't understand," replied the rabbi. "I cannot forgive them, for they did not insult me, the rabbi of Brisk. They insulted a common man, a poor man. I cannot forgive on behalf of that man. If they want forgiveness, let them go to that poor man and ask it."

And Rabbi Heschel concluded by saying: "During the Holocaust, when a million Jewish children were slaughtered, I was comfortable in Cincinnati. I was warm and ate three meals a day, and no one humiliated me, no one oppressed me. If one of those children wants to forgive the Nazis, that child can. But I cannot forgive on that child's behalf.

That was Rabbi Heschel, never forgetting the hurt, the grief, the deprivation of the other; not being willing to "forgive and forget" and to rationalize that everything is alright, but constantly crying out against injustice and suffering when inflicted on others. *Ashrei hador,* blessed is the generation that had the priviledge of this great man in its midst, and may we prove worthy of his teaching.

3

Notes on a Friendship
Abraham Joshua Heschel and Reinhold Niebuhr

URSULA M. NIEBUHR

Before embarking on my assignment, I would like to ask you to realize how difficult it is to describe a friendship. How can I, how can anyone, describe a relationship between two people without being both subjective and somewhat impressionistic? For, after all, I have no body of literary evidence. There is not a corpus of letters between Abraham Joshua Heschel and my husband, Reinhold Niebuhr, so there is no "hard data," in the lingo of today.

There is no body of letters. My husband was not a letter writer, nor was he a letter keeper. As he was largely his own secretary, and answered his own letters, unless they were on official Seminary business, he would, as he was no conscientious keeper of letters, just throw them away! I do not know how many letters were thus lost. If a letter came from a friend whom we shared, then he would bring it home for me to see. Then *I* would keep it.

So, I was lucky enough to keep and to cherish two letters from Abraham to Reinhold. One was a brief note from Rome, undated, but I think we are able to date it September 1964. It ended thus, "We are meeting with friends in the Vatican. And scheduled to see the Pope tomorrow. Thinking of you with affection and hope you are feeling better." Then both of us got letters from him, when he was in Florida, in March 1970, convalescing after a heart attack and a bout of hepatitis. He addressed Reinhold as "Beloved and revered friend." (I was merely "Dear Ursula." But I *did* get a letter all to myself!) He thought that the climate of Florida, which had so benefited him, might be good for Reinhold, and that was the reason he had written to me too. In his letter to Reinhold he wrote that he was feeling so much better, which made him feel he could write a "pleasant letter, informing you [Reinhold] of my own recovery as an example, precedent and in anticipation of hearing of your recovery." He continued, "Such good news from you is what I pray for daily. You are so deeply ingrained in my thoughts, and I am eager to renew our walking and talking together on Riverside Drive." He went on, "Miami Beach may be intellectually America's Siberia, still the climate has proved beneficial." And he continued, pressing Reinhold to think of coming to Florida.

So much for the written record. There are brief notes inscribed on articles which he gave us, but there are no more letters.

So what is my material? Memory, which proverbially is a fickle jade. Yet because Abraham was so special, so memorable, I dare to share these memories with you.

I do not know when Reinhold first met Abraham. I think I had that pleasure before he did. One of my Barnard College students was married to a rabbinical student at the Jewish Theological Seminary. She told me about the wonderful teacher her husband had and kindly asked me to tea so that I might meet him. I was, of course, entranced at the prospect, and by the occasion. I shall never forget that afternoon on lower Claremont Avenue, and I remember reporting to Reinhold on both the occasion and this fabulous person I met.

I remember also that, in the early '50s, I kept copies of Abraham's *The Earth Is the Lord's* and *The Sabbath,* which I had ordered for our department, in my office at Barnard College. The jackets of both were pinned up on a big board with other topical items outside my office. Many students and colleagues would note these and come in to chat and look at these books. Reinhold and I also kept our own personal copies of Abraham's books at home. One of these, a second printing of *The Earth Is the Lord's* is, I noticed recently, inscribed rather formally to "Dr. Reinhold Niebuhr, in friendship and esteem," dated 1952.

It was in February of that year that my husband suffered the first of many strokes. He was out of action for some months, and I am inclined to think he and Abraham did not get to know each other well until somewhat later.

In the middle or later '50s, Reinhold read a paper to the annual joint meeting of the faculties of the Jewish Theological Seminary and Union Theological Seminary. It was later published in the volume *Pious and Secular America,* 1958. This paper, entitled "The Relations of Christians and Jews in Western Civilization," analyzed the differences between the two traditions in terms of universalism and particularism; of law and grace; of messianism and so forth. He repeated his long-held conviction that Christians should not evangelize their Jewish brethren. Also, he spoke with hope and gratitude for the State of Israel.

This paper was well received, and it may have accelerated the friendship between him and Abraham. By the time Reinhold retired from Union Seminary in 1960, they had become good friends. For the last 12 years or so of his life, Abraham really was my husband's closest friend.

As I have already mentioned, Reinhold had suffered a succession of strokes from 1952 on. These, although not affecting his speech or his mind, luckily, had nevertheless weakened his general health. It also had made him more stationary, and although we had some splendid years away, when he was Visiting Professor at Harvard and then at Princeton (also an earlier year when we were at the Institute for Advanced Studies at Princeton) he was no longer criss-crossing the country, or going abroad. Abraham, however, was; and, reporting on his travels and on his meetings with different groups of people in the universities as he spoke around the country, he brought that world back to Reinhold, and he would share with him his reactions as to people and the situation in the world outside.

Thus, the civil rights movement, and Abraham's support of, and friendship with, Martin Luther King, formed the subject matter of much conversation between the two of them. I remember so well his telling us about Selma. He was shocked, deeply, to see white southern women spitting on and yelling at the Catholic nuns with whom he walked, and often would refer to that experience. When riots in Harlem followed the death of Martin Luther King, he went with other religious leaders to see the mayor of New York. He spoke to us about this occasion, but others, such as Dr. John Bennett, told us of the profound impression made by Abraham's simple question: How could one pray when such a situation as in Harlem existed?

A week after the bombing of the Baptist Church in Birmingham on September 15, 1963, when four children were murdered, my husband and James Baldwin took part in a television program in New York.

There was a regular Sunday program sponsored by the Protestant
Council of New York, and usually the host was a well-known minister
of a well-known Madison Avenue Protestant church. On this
occasion, he excused himself, as he had been abroad, and did not feel
up-to-date on situations and issues. So, luckily, as so many of us
thought, his place was taken by Dr. Thomas Kilgore, Jr., minister of
the Friendship Baptist Church, and the New York Director for the
Southern Leadership Conference. I do not know if Abraham listened
to the discussion, which to me was appropriate to the tragedy being
considered, but I do remember Reinhold and Abraham talking about
it later. For this was the world where both of them lived their faith.
Reinhold, not in good health, now had to watch from the sidelines.
Abraham, although himself frail, was carrying the ball for him, and
for many others as well.

Likewise, with the religious coalition against the war in Vietnam,
many were the exchanges I caught echoes of, for most of their conversations were when the two of them were together. Sometimes I might join, either their walking and talking on Riverside Drive,
or I would come back home and find Abraham chatting with
Reinhold. I am sure Sylvia Heschel had the same experience as I.
Sometimes I wished I had overheard more, but Reinhold would tell
me what they had talked about and always with great satisfaction.

In the letter from which I have already quoted, Abraham wrote to
Reinhold: "You are deeply ingrained in my thought, and I am eager to
renew our walking and talking on Riverside Drive." This is how I see
the two of them in my memory, as I am sure Sylvia also does. The
Heschels lived at 425 Riverside Drive and we, after Reinhold retired
from Union Seminary in 1960, lived at 404, so we were only a couple
of blocks apart. These walks, ordered by the doctor for Reinhold's
health, when in the company of Abraham, became times of exchange
and refreshment. As Reinhold's own strength decreased in the later
'60s, he became rather more obviously lame on his left side. I would
watch them—Reinhold over six feet, leaning a bit like the Tower of
Pisa, and Abraham, himself not too strong, and a good deal shorter—
and wonder if Abraham would be able to hold Reinhold up if he
tilted! One of our devoted doormen at 404 worried, as I often did,
when they started. When I came in, he would alert me and I would go
down Riverside Drive looking for them. Luckily, Reinhold never did
tilt or tumble, but I still have a vivid picture of those two dear figures
happily talking to each other with their different architectural
conformations.

I would like, now, to focus on one phrase Abraham used in that
letter: "You are so deeply ingrained in my thoughts." The two were

very congenial in their thought, and in different contexts and different fashions one often echoed the thought of the other.

This is strikingly illustrated by their common use of the words "mystery" and "meaning." Long before we had the pleasure of knowing Abraham, Reinhold had written and spoken about the mystery of life and the part that faith, and different systems of faith, played in trying to bring meaning into the mystery of the self; into the mystery of creation and the mystery of transcendence. In his inimitable way, as a poet, Abraham expressed this succinctly and vividly: "Is not the human face a living mixture of mystery and meaning?"[1]

Reinhold had written two essays at different times, both entitled "Mystery and Meaning." The first he wrote in 1945, which was published the next year in the volume *Discerning the Signs of the Times: Sermons for Today and Tomorrow,* and the other one was written much later, based on sermons which he had preached at Harvard and at Union Seminary and published in the volume *Pious and Secular America,* 1958. I noted a few characteristic sentences: "We live our life in various realms of meaning, which do not quite cohere rationally. Our meanings are surrounded by a penumbra of mystery, which is not penetrated by reason."[2] Or again: "Faith resolves the mystery of life by the mystery of God. . . . All known existence points beyond itself. To realize that it points beyond itself to God is to assert that the mystery of life does not resolve life into meaninglessness."[3] In this same essay, Reinhold continued:

> The sense of both mystery and meaning is perhaps most succinctly expressed in the 45th chapter of Isaiah where, practically in the same breath, the prophet declares on the one hand, "Verily thou are a God that hidest thyself, O God of Israel, the Saviour," and on the other, insists that God has made himself known: "I have not spoken in secret, in a dark place of the earth: I said not unto the seed of Jacob, Seek ye me in vain: I the Lord speak righteousness, I declare things that are right." This double emphasis is a perfect symbolic expression both of the meaning that faith discerns and of the penumbra of mystery it recognizes around the core of meaning.[4]

The theme of "mystery and meaning" likewise was central in Abraham's thought, as all of us know well. "It is in the awareness that the mystery we face is incomparably deeper than we know that all creative thinking begins," he wrote.[5] Or again: "To maintain the right balance of mystery and meaning, of stillness and utterance, of reverence and action seems to be the goal of religious existence."[6] Or yet again: "Sensitivity to the mystery of living is the essence of human dignity. It is the soil in which our consciousness has its roots, and out of which a sense of meaning is derived. Man does not live by explanations alone, but by the sense of wonder and mystery."[7]

It was no wonder to me that these two friends found each other so congenial, not only in this shared universe of discourse, but also in their dependence upon and reference to the Hebrew prophets. Reinhold always emphasized that it was the prophetic vision of the transcendent righteousness of God that gave both the standard and the dynamic for ethical action. It was the eighth- and sixth-century prophets who inspired my husband's thought and work in the field of social ethics. And we all know, of course, that it was the study of these very same prophets which served as the foundation of Abraham's entire religious world-view and spurred him into a life of prophetic action. Abraham's great book on the prophets, Reinhold and I agreed, should be required reading for every minister and teacher. Before I had read the book, talking about Abraham with my husband, I had said, "Is he not a prophet of Israel?" But then we did not think his appearance was angular enough!—as we had imagined the prophets to be. Reinhold replied, "Perhaps he is too benign in his character." Yet, in the introduction to that book, Abraham writes: "Prophecy is a sham unless it is experienced as a word of God swooping down on man and converting him into a prophet."[8] I think others would agree with me that the word of God had indeed "swooped down" on these two friends.

Recently a young church historian sent me a couple of pamphlets issued during the First World War and published by the War Welfare Commission of the Evangelical Synod, the denomination in which my husband was brought up and in which he served. (Afterwards, it became part of the United Church of Christ.) Reinhold had not been accepted as a chaplain owing to a heart murmur, but he was used as a sort of chaplain to chaplains, whom he visited and kept in touch with in the military camps in this country. There was a short column by Reinhold in one of the pamphlets with the title "Imitating God." As I read it, I thought to myself "I think Abraham would have approved of this." Reinhold wrote:

Imitate God? . . . Our minds will not compass the universe or comprehend its mysteries as does the mind of God, but we can imitate his ability to look into the souls of men. . . . Then too, we can imitate the holiness of God. We will never achieve it. . . . It sets a goal before us that can never be reached and that therefore always keeps us striving.

Somehow, this reminded me of the words of Abraham:

Man may act in the likeness of God. . . . To live in such likeness is the essence of imitation of the Divine. . . . We live by the conviction that acts of goodness reflect the hidden light of His holiness. . . . The goal is that man be *transformed;* to worship the Holy in order to be holy.[9]

Observing, and now remembering, the friendship between these two men, I realize that it was the extraordinary openness in exchange with others that made Abraham such a unique person and unique friend. Was this a gift, a particular grace that was given him? So we might think, yet in his utterances it was this quality that to him was part of biblical religion. "The demand, as understood in biblical religion, is to be alert and to be open to what is happening."[10] Abraham was all of one piece, his manner of meeting others, of listening to them, his interest was all part of his belief about life. I am reminded, as no doubt others have been, of the remark of Loren Eisley: "The habit of prayer, by which I mean the habit of listening." Abraham *listened* to his friends, to those who needed understanding and support, whether individuals or groups, and he listened to God, to the word of God. "The habit of listening" was for him indeed "the habit of prayer." Again and again the relationship of the transcendent to the immediate happenings of historic existence, these were noted not only in his writing but in his actions. There was a transcendent meaning in the necessary actions of daily life, so he reminded us again and again. "Awe enables us . . . to sense in small things the beginnings of infinite significance, to sense the ultimate in the common and the simple."[11]

But I have said enough. As Abraham might say, "May I tell you a story?" I really want to tell two stories. One day in early spring, when the fallen snow had become a horrid, muddy flood, swooping round the corners of the streets, I was approaching 122nd Street off Broadway. I saw two figures whom I recognized, coming from different directions. One was a gentleman who was my hairdresser, Mr. Aris. When I had first heard about him, I had thought he was Mr. Harris, but he might have dropped the "H". He turned out to be, however, a Greek, from the Island of Crete. The other figure was Abraham Joshua Heschel, who was just back from Jerusalem. (I think it was the time when he came back with his beard!) All three of us converged, trying to leap across the particularly dirty, muddy mess which was characteristic of New York in the meltingness after a snowfall. I was greeted by both gentlemen, and grasping the leashes of my two poodles firmly, I introduced them to each other, Rabbi Heschel and Mr. Aris. Suddenly remembering, Tertullian's rhetorical question, "What has Jerusalem to do with Athens?" I told Abraham that Mr. Aris had just returned from Greece, but had been born in Crete. "Ah," said Abraham, "the birthplace of Zeus." This hit a bull's eye, and Mr. Aris was enchanted, and asked Abraham if he had been to Crete. I was too busy trying to control the poodles and not get completely drowned in the mud to remember what happened, but I do remember the choreography of that meeting where there was a tremendous amount of interest shown by Abraham, very characteristically, in the background of Mr. Aris—What was he doing, and how did he like living in America, and all the rest. Both gentlemen told me afterwards that they had so enjoyed the meeting. Although there is nothing very much to this story, somehow it seemed to me so characteristic of Abraham.

The other story connects with one of the letters I had mentioned earlier. On a lovely Friday afternoon, my husband and I returned to our apartment house after a walk along Riverside Drive. Our very pleasant doorman told us that our friend had dropped in, and on learning we were out had left with him a gift for us. The doorman took this from some safe place and presented us with a bottle, wrapped in silver foil. We asked whether he knew who had left it. He answered that it was the learned gentleman with whom Professor Niebuhr walks. I triumphantly exclaimed, "Abraham, no doubt!" The doorman continued, "He said he had just come back from Rome, and that he had seen the Pope." I am afraid I let out a somewhat unladylike cry of glee, and said, "Heavens! This must be holy water!" We went into the elevator and upstairs. Entering our apartment, and while helping my husband off with his coat, he said to me, "You must ring Abraham up at once and thank him." I looked out of the window across the Hudson where the sun had dropped behind the horizon of New Jersey. I said, "I don't think I should, the sun has set and Shabbat has started." At that moment, the telephone rang. It was Abraham, "I'm back. Have you got my present? It is brandy for Reinhold. And I did see the Pope." "Abraham," I squealed, "I was going to ring you up to thank you, Reinhold is right here, but the sun has set; so of course I didn't." "It is all right. There are two more minutes to go, and I wanted to be sure. I'll see you soon. My love to you both."

Notes

1. Abraham Joshua Heschel, *Who Is Man?* (Stanford, CA: Stanford University Press, 1965), p. 38.
2. Reinhold Niebuhr, *Pious and Secular America* (New York: Charles Scribner's Sons, 1958), p. 123.
3. Reinhold Niebuhr, *Discerning the Signs of the Times: Sermons for Today and Tomorrow* (New York: Charles Scribner's Sons, 1946).
4. *Ibid.*
5. Abraham Joshua Heschel, *God In Search of Man: A Philosophy of Judaism* (New York: Farrar, Straus and Cudahy, 1955), p. 115. Hereafter cited as *Search.*
6. Abraham Joshua Heschel, *The Insecurity of Freedom: Essays on Human Existence* (New York: Schocken Books, 1966), p. 123.
7. *Ibid.*, pp. 123–124.
8. Abraham Joshua Heschel, *The Prophets* (New York: Harper and Row, 1962), p. xiv.
9. *Search,* pp. 289–290, 311.
10. *Who Is Man?*, pp. 115–116.
11. *Search,* p. 75.

PART
TWO

Heschel as Biblical Theologian

4

Coexistence With God
Heschel's Exposition of Biblical Theology

BERNHARD W. ANDERSON

Biblical interpretation in the twentieth century has been influenced profoundly by a splendid line of Jewish thinkers, among whom may be named Franz Rosenzweig, Martin Buber, Will Herberg, and Abraham Joshua Heschel. None of these men were biblical theologians in the proper sense. Each understood himself to be a philosopher of religion, and specifically a philosopher of Judaism. Nevertheless, all of them in one degree or another have taken the Bible seriously—and of course I refer to the Hebrew Bible, which in Christian circles is called the Old Testament. This was especially true of Heschel, a powerful representative of that renaissance of Jewish life and thought known as the Hasidic movement. "Judaism," he boldly declared, "is a confrontation with the Bible, and a philosophy of Judaism must be a confrontation with the thought of the Bible."[1]

My assignment is to consider Heschel's understanding of biblical theology, that is, his explication and exposition of the faith of the believing and worshiping community as expressed in the tripartite

47

canon of the Hebrew Bible: Torah (Pentateuch), Nebi'im (Prophets), and Kethubim (Writings) or, to use the Jewish acronymn, TaNaK. Once I described Will Herberg as a biblical theologian, and that was a bold venture.[2] In this symposium on the life and thought of Heschel, however, I face an even greater difficulty. Unfortunately I did not have the privilege of knowing Rabbi Heschel personally, except through casual contacts such as a civil rights march in Alabama or a Festschrift dinner in honor of James Muilenburg at Union Theological Seminary. In retrospect, I wish that I could have found the opportunity to converse theologically with him face to face, as I did with Will Herberg in our *Tischreden*. It was through the written word that Heschel made a personal impact—and I hasten to add, a profound and forceful impact.

In this case, relationship through the written word has special difficulties. For one thing, Heschel's poetic literary style is unusual in the fields of philosophy and theology—disciplines which traditionally have relied heavily upon analytic, discursive reasoning. Heschel's style, in its own way, is probing and illuminating and, indeed, is eminently suited for a philosophical venture into "the meaning beyond the mystery." Readers, however, find themselves enthralled by elegant literary formulations which, if I may use his own simile as a tribute, are "like brooks that hold the sky." Again and again I have paused over a sentence as though it were a thing of beauty in itself or have been arrested by an aphorism that claims to be a context unto itself, separable like a gem from the setting in which it is clasped. Moreover, Heschel's writing is interlaced with duplications and recapitulations, in the manner of a Mozart who echoes phrases, repeats sections, or reuses whole cadences in his artistic expression. This kind of literary elaboration is appropriate to the philosophical task as Heschel conceives it.[3] Nevertheless, it is difficult to summarize and analyze the thought of this poetic philosopher, not only for the reasons given but because of the rich, diverse literary output of his career. We are grateful to Fritz Rothschild, above all, who has provided us with a masterful introduction to, and compilation of, Heschel's writings under the title, *Between God and Man: An Interpretation of Judaism* (1959, 1975). A compliment to this book would be to say that the relationship between Rothschild and Heschel is on the analogy of Baruch to the Prophet.

In view of all of this, how does one go about the task of setting forth Heschel's view of biblical theology? Certainly I do not claim to have read everything that Heschel has written; and such encyclopedic knowledge, even if I had it, would not necessarily help. As a biblical scholar I am tempted to turn to his monumental work on *The Prophets,* basically his doctoral dissertation at the University of Berlin (1933) which appeared in expanded form (1962) at the height of his career. I have decided, however, after some hesitation to turn instead to his book, *God In Search of Man* (1955). This book, the companion volume to his earlier work on the philosophy of religion *Man Is Not Alone* (1951), builds on his study of Israelite prophecy but deals with prophetic revelation in the broad horizon of biblical theology. Here he deals not just with the philosophy of religion but the philosophy of Judaism, that is, the God who is known through the biblical revelation and the response to that revelation in terms of covenantal coexistence or "partnership with God." Concentrating on this book, with side-references to other writings, will have the further advantage of allowing Heschel himself to provide the outline of thought, rather than proceeding on the basis of a synthesis provided by others.[4]

In this book Heschel maintains that there are three dimensions of biblical faith, or I should say, existence in faith—for he is always aware of the involvement of the modern person in the biblical drama. Each of these interrelated dimensions he appropriately signifies by citing a biblical verse. First, a quotation from Isaiah 40:26 which invites one to contemplate the wonder and mystery of the world: "Lift up your eyes on high and see who created these!" Second, a quotation from the Exodus-Sinai story—the opening of the Decalogue in Exodus 20:2 which refers to the God specifically known and worshiped in Israel: "I am Adonai [Yahweh], thy God. . . ." And finally, the citation of Exodus 24:7, a passage which appears in the context of a covenant ceremony in which the people pledge to respond in action and lifestyle: "We shall do and we shall hear." Following Heschel's lead, let us explore these three dimensions of biblical theology.

The Sense of the Holy

The starting point in the explication and elaboration of the faith of the believing and worshiping community as expressed in the literature of the Bible is the sense of the holy—a religious awareness that the Israelite religion has in common, to some degree, with other religions and with general human consciousness. The "idea" or, better, the awareness of the Holy, to recall the classical study by Rudolf Otto, is "otherworldly" in the sense that the Holy is beyond the conceptual categories of this world or the familiar realities of everyday life.[5] In biblical perspective, however (and this is an important difference from Otto), the Holy is not just a state of consciousness. Rather, the Holy is Power—Power that has its source beyond this world but that becomes manifest in the human world as redemptive concern and ethical demand.

Attempting to find a point of contact between the biblical witness to the experience of the Holy and general (even modern) human consciousness, Heschel starts at the basic level of the divine-human encounter: the sense of the sublime. "There is no faith at first sight," he says in a memorable line (p. 152)—referring, of course, to faith in the God identified in the Bible. To use a liturgical figure, one can approach the Temple, where the presence of God is celebrated, only through the outer court, that is, through a human sense of the sublime which is manifest in spontaneous awe and radical amazement. With all the literary powers at his command, Heschel attempts to appeal to the sense of the sublime or, we might say, "the lost sense" of the holy. In one poetically inspired passage Heschel writes:

> Awe enables us to perceive in the world intimations of the divine, to sense in small things the beginning of infinite significance, to sense the ultimate in the common and the simple; to feel in the rush of the passing the stillness of the eternal (p. 75).

The sense of the sublime, however, has been lost only in the sense that it is dormant at the basic level of human existence, like a sleeping princess that waits to be reawakened. Human beings, according to Heschel, are so constituted that they cannot escape moments of wonder that things are, rather than are not ("stand still and consider"). Existentially, a sensitive person senses the marvel in the smallest things and is prompted to raise the ultimate question about one's place in the world and the meaning of the vast cosmic whole. Life is a quest but—in Heschel's view—only because human beings respond, whether they realize it or not, to a question that is put to them from beyond the world. The questing initiative comes from the God who is beyond the human world, who transcends all the categories of human thought and all the dimensions of human experience, and yet who— *mirabile dictu*—enters into the human world with redemptive concern and ethical demand. The human quest for God is, after all, a reflex of God's quest for humanity. "All human history as described in the Bible," Heschel writes, "may be summarized in one phrase: *God is in search of man*" (p. 136).

At this point, Heschel stands on the boundary between the Bible and the modern world. He is both a theologian and an apologist—a double role that devolves upon a philosopher who stands in the circle of faith. In another context he speaks of this enterprise as "depth theology."[6] This is an eminently fitting term, insofar as the philosopher is concerned to establish a meeting-point between the divine initiative and human searching, as "deep calls unto deep" (Ps. 42:7). Methodologically, however, Heschel does not begin with the world or with the subjectivity of human experience but with the God who is beyond and who is nevertheless concerned about, and involved with, humanity. "It is the mystery that evokes our religious concern," he says, "and it is the mystery where religious thinking must begin" (p. 114). He goes on to say that, traditionally, thinking about God has been *via eminentia*, that is, a movement from the known to the unknown. Heschel's starting point, on the other hand, is "the unknown within the known, the infinite within the finite, the mystery within the order" (p. 114).

Accordingly, Heschel takes with philosophical seriousness a basic biblical datum: The God who speaks through the Bible is not a phenomenon of this world. To domesticate God within the human world would be to commit the fundamental apostasy of the Golden Calf: the worship of a god who is a contrived idol of the imagination, e.g., an ideology of a social group or nation, or the subjective fancy of the "heart." Heschel's radical sense of divine transcendence prompts him to make statements that, on first consideration, sound like those of a mystic. "The living encounter with reality," he writes, "takes place on a level that precedes conceptualization, on a level that is responsive, *immediate, preconceptual,* and *presymbolic*" (p. 115). This view of a wordless encounter, an ecstatic experience beyond expression, seems to conflict with what Heschel says in other contexts about God's revelation through human words (a matter to which we shall return later). Here, however, he is talking to those who are still standing in the forecourt of the temple—those for whom the sense of wonder is the inescapable basis of all human conceptuality and symbolism. At this level the sense of the holy is inarticulate: a song without words. The world may be "an allusion to God" (p. 78), but in the presence of the holy "all language is inaccurate" and "silence is preferable to speech" (p. 123).

Even in this context Heschel slightly qualifies statements about the inadequacy of human language. "Words are not indispensable to cognition," he writes; but they are "necessary when we wish to communicate our ideas to others" (p. 123). One wonders, however, whether words, especially inspired, poetic words, are also necessary in the sharing and communication of faith, and hence, are indispensable in expressing those revelatory events which constitute a community in relation to God. It is clear, however, that Heschel's main attack is directed against rationalists who suppose that God, if there be a God, can be captured in human thought; and he also rejects the claim of some linguistic philosophers that language is "the house of being" (Heidegger). "Concepts, words must not become screens; they must be regarded as windows" (p. 116) that are open to the beyond.

The conclusion is, as Heschel states it, that "God is an ontological presupposition"; hence, all statements made about God are "understatements" (p. 123). The inadequacy of human language and conceptuality is the corollary of the sense of the holy—that elemental sense of the ineffable which is native to human being as such, and which surfaces in moments of awe and wonder when one stands before the ultimate question (and unknowingly, before the Ultimate Questioner). This only means, however, that faith is not something alien to human existence, a venture into a realm that is irrational. In a profound sense it is the human answer to the ultimate question that God asks, and hence, a "return to God" ("repentance" in the prophetic sense). In an exquisite passage, Heschel writes:

> We do not have to discover the world of faith; we only have to recover it. It is not a *terra incognita,* an unknown land; it is a forgotten land, and our relation to God is a palimpsest rather than a *tabula rasa* (p. 141).

The latter figure is particularly striking to a biblical scholar. A palimpsest, of course, is a parchment document that has been rubbed over two or three times so that a new inscription may be made on it, but the previous writing has not been completely erased and therefore is still visible to some degree and capable of being restored. So it is analogically. Human existence is not a blank tablet, but a palimpsest which, at the fundamental ontological level, is imprinted with a native sense of awe and wonder. In this sense, faith is the recoverable basis of human life. As Heschel puts it, speaking out of and to the Jewish community, "every one of us has stood at the foot of Sinai" (p. 141) in the presence of the Holy God who speaks and calls for us to answer. And this can be true of any sensitive person. "Only in moments when we are able to share in the spirit of awe that fills the world are we able to understand what happened to Israel at Sinai" (p. 196).

Divine Revelation

We turn now to a second dimension of Heschel's exposition of biblical theology: divine revelation. To the average person, he points out, "revelation is a sort of mental outcast," hardly worthy of acceptance in respectable society; and this is true also, I may add, for many biblical scholars and theologians today. Yet for Heschel this subject, which eludes scientific inquiry, is centrally important. It is the logical and theological sequel to his discussion of God as the ontological presupposition of human existence.

He makes this point in a discussion that opens with a quotation from Psalm 19: "The heavens declare the glory of God." Human beings, says Heschel, are "confronted with a world that alludes to something beyond itself. . . . and it is that allusiveness which conveys to us the awareness of a spiritual dimension of reality, the relatedness of being to transcendent meaning" (p. 108). He goes on to say that "the mystery of meaning is silent." As the psalmist says, "there is no speech, nor are there words; their voice is not heard." This means that "beyond our reasoning and beyond our believing, there is a *preconceptual* faculty that senses the glory, the presence of the Divine." But something more is needed than this.

> The answer to the ultimate question is not found in the notion that the foundations of the world lie amid impenetrable fog. Fog is no substitute for light, and the totally unknown God is not a god but a name for the cosmic darkness. The God whose presence in the world we sense is anonymous, mysterious (p. 108).

We may sense that God *is*, but not know what, or who, God is. Fundamental questions arise: What is God's name (i.e., identity)? What is God's relation to the world and to people? What is God's will and how should people worship (i.e., "serve") God? Heschel concludes by saying: "The sense of wonder, awe, and mystery is necessary, but not sufficient to find the way from wonder to worship, from willingness to realization, from awe to action" (p. 108). In other words, if I may put it this way, Psalm 19A is a torso by itself; its thought must be completed with Psalm 19B which praises the God whose will is revealed in the Torah.

It is the Bible, Heschel affirms, that enables one to move from the world to knowledge of the God who is beyond the mystery of the world. Through the Bible, the God, who remains invisible in the world, becomes audible. God has spoken, and God speaks. In this context, language is considered from a different angle than when Heschel was criticizing the attempt to imprison God in the categories of human rationality. The Bible, he says, is "holiness in words," that is, these human words are the vehicles that God *uses* to establish relations with a people. "It is as if God took these Hebrew words and breathed into them of His power, and the words became a live wire charged with His spirit. To this very day they are hyphens between heaven and earth" (p. 244). How easy it is to speak with disdain of "words, words, words," as does an actor in one of Shakespeare's plays; yet strange as it may seem "the light of God" is "given in the form of language." Heschel writes: "This is the distinction of the Bible: on the highest level of radical amazement, where all expression ends, it gives us the word" (p. 250). Heschel has no sympathy with the biblical literalist—the kind of reader, as he says with wry humor, "who, when you talk to him of Jacob's ladder, would ask the number of the steps" (p. 182). To understand biblical expressions, like the phrase "God spoke," the theologian must consider that in the language of faith, words are often used poetically with various levels of meaning, that often words do not function descriptively to evoke preconceived meanings, but they have an indicative function, intimating "something which we intuit but cannot fully comprehend." Heschel has provided the foundation for a biblical theology of language (especially, chap. 18), and specifically, for understanding that the Bible is the Word of God in human words.[7]

Revelation, understood as God's communication with human beings, must be understood in dramatic terms. Indeed, drama is a key term in Heschel's discussion. "The Bible," he says, "is not a book to be read but a drama in which to participate" (p. 254). In this drama, it is God who takes the initiative. It is God who turns toward humanity in the first instance, inviting a response, and hence, the movement is the opposite of the mystic experience of a human being turning to God. "The episodes recorded in the Bible to the discerning eye are episodes of one great drama: the quest of God for man; His search for man, and man's flight from Him" (p. 197).

The metaphor of drama helps us to understand what occurs in the event of revelation. Heschel is emphatic in stating that revelation is *not* a disclosure of God's being; *not* the divine essence or nature, timeless qualities of goodness, perfection, immutability, and so on; and certainly revelation is *not* the communication of ideas in the syntax of Hebrew grammar, as some Protestant divines have supposed. The being of God is inaccessible; and even in the moment of revelation,

God is never an object of thought. What is revealed in the Bible, as Heschel puts it, is "God's relation to history," not God's "very Self" (p. 261). As in a drama, God is known only on the basis of actions that establish relations and challenge a human response.

This emphasis on the *revealed relationship* between God and human beings opens up new horizons in biblical theology. We have already said that, in Heschel's view, God is concealed in the world and that concealment is not lifted even in the moment of revelation. As we read in the Sinai story, no human being can see God and live (Ex. 33:20); only God's voice can be heard. This Voice, however, is one that speaks in tones of concern for human beings. Human beings are the center of God's attention and interest. From the human point of view, this evokes the response of awe which may have one of two reactions: either an attempt to flee from God into idolatry, or the grateful pledge of obedience to the divine will and the exercise of responsibility as the representative of God on earth. The human question is raised in an attitude of wonder in Psalm 8 and it is raised by one who wished to be a fugitive from God's presence in Job, chapter 7.

> What are human beings that you consider them,
> > human persons that you seek them out?   (Psalm 8:4;
> > cf. Job 7:17)

There are various aspects of the experienced relationship of divine concern. For one thing, revelation is not only a call to coexist but to co-participate with God in the historical drama. "Revelation means," says Heschel, "that the thick silence which fills the endless distance between God and the human mind was pierced." People came to realize that God is concerned with human affairs. But more: "Not only does man need God, God is also in need of man" (p. 196). To this intriguing notion of "God's need" we shall return later. There is another dimension of divine concern, however, and that is the divine pathos—a subject that Heschel has explored creatively in his great work on the prophets. Here I shall refrain from dealing with this important subject at length, realizing that it will receive deserved attention in another essay in this symposium. Suffice it to say that the God who is revealed in relation to human history, and in particular to the history of Israel, is the God who takes people seriously and passionately—with the passion of indignation about human wrongs, the passion of anguish about human failure and hardheartedness, the passion of sorrow at the dreadful consequences of human actions. Unlike the God of the Greek philosophers who transcends the mundane sphere of change and suffering, and who is apathetic (without passion), the God of the Bible is the God who, as the transcendent Creator, chooses to become involved in the human drama. A prophet, like Jeremiah, is one who is so in tune with—so sympathetic with—the divine pathos of involvement in the human drama that his words have the forceful passion of the word of God; and his "passion story" of suffering and rejection is a metaphor of God's pathos in dealing with the people. A sense of mystery is common to all peoples, Heschel points out, but the Bible discloses a special mystery: the pathos of the God who is involved in the human drama.

This drama of God's involvement with human beings, and especially the people Israel, is related to historical events—unique events that happened long ago, the wonder of which survives into the present. At this point, Heschel enters a debate in the field of biblical theology that has been going on in the past generation and that continues into the present—and which will probably survive into the next century if the end does not come precipitously in the form of an atomic holocaust. The question for debate in academic halls has been whether the biblical drama is only a story that makes an esthetic appeal, or whether it is in some sense a history rooted in events that occurred in the experience of a people. Heschel, if I understand him rightly, seems to throw this ball to the biblical theologians, on the assumption that a distinction is to be made between the Torah as witness to the mystery of God's presence in human history and the Torah as a witness to historical facts. Philosophy of religion, he says in regard to the Pentateuch must deal with biblical literature at the level of "grandeur and amazement"; theology, however, must deal with the Bible as a historical document and consider historical questions (p. 258). If I were to meet Rabbi Heschel in an eschatological situation, beyond the boundaries of this world, that would be one of the first questions that I would like to discuss with him!

Despite ambiguities on this point, Heschel affirms that the revelation of God, expressed through the words of Scripture, was mediated through events that happened in the past. Indeed, he directs one of his major tirades against religions or philosophies which have a "contempt for time" and which devaluate the category of the individual and unique. "At night—in the soul—all moments look alike," he says. "Yet Jewish tradition claims that there is a hierarchy of moments within time, that all ages are not alike" (p. 205). Some times are unique, not only because of their historical concreteness, but because of their intimate relation to God. These events, in the faith of a believing and worshiping community, are to be remembered and celebrated. Revelation, he insists, is grounded in "unique events that happened at particular moments of history" (p. 196). Indeed, "To believe is to remember."

It is not surprising, then, that Heschel—in anticipation of the recent emergence of so-called "narrative theology"—put great emphasis on the *haggadic,* or story-telling, dimension of the Bible. A fatal error was made, he points out, when the translators of the Greek Bible, the Septuagint, rendered the Hebrew term *torah* ("guidance," "instruction") with the Greek *nomos,* which means "law." The halachic or legal portions of the Bible are exceedingly important, as we shall see; indeed, "the interrelationship of halacha and agada [haggadah] is the very heart of Judaism. Halacha without agada is dead, agada without halacha is wild" (p. 337). He insists, however, that ultimately the torah-law is dependent on the torah-story. "The event at Sinai, the mystery of revelation, belongs to the sphere of agada," which indicates that the law derives its authority and its motivation from the drama of God's turning toward a people (p. 338).

Biblical theologians will raise the question as to whether Heschel, even when stressing the primacy of narrative, is influenced by the halachic spirit of Judaism. In the book under discussion he rarely pauses to reflect on "the saving experience" of the Exodus, as does Emil Fackenheim in his little book, *God's Presence in History*, or as does Martin Buber, whom Fackenheim cites in his philosophical reflection on the miracle at the Sea.[8] It is Sinai, the narrative of the commanding Voice, that engages Heschel's philosophical attention. Even so, in good Hasidic spirit he resists the anti-narrative attitude that has dominated Judaism at times. As an example of this negative attitude he cites a classical rabbinic question found at the outset of Rashi's commentary on Genesis. Rashi quotes a judgment by Rabbi Isaac: "The Torah should have commenced with chapter 12 of Exodus"—for, of course, before that point there are scarcely any laws. Heschel comments:

> The premise and implications of this question are staggering. The Bible should have omitted such non-legal chapters as those on creation, the sins of Adam and Cain, the flood, the tower of Babel, the lives of Abraham, Isaac, and Jacob, the lives of the twelve tribes, the suffering and miracles in Egypt! (p. 328).

God's revelation, then, is presented in story form. This story prevents revelation from being reduced to ancient history. There are many events which are dead and gone, and we are liberated from the past. "On the other hand, there are events which never become past, . . . events of hoary antiquity" that "hold us in their spell to this very day" (p. 211). The biblical story, above all, conveys the meaning of such events and therefore has a dimension of dramatic contemporaneity. "Sacred history," Heschel says, "may be described as an attempt to overcome the dividing line of past and present, as an attempt *to see the past in the present tense*" (p. 211–212). When read in faith, the Bible is a drama of the divine–human encounter.

Human Response

This leads us to the final dimension of Heschel's exposition of biblical theology: response to the divine overture. "The Bible is more than the word of God," he writes; "it is the word of God *and* man" (p. 260). This interrelationship, this co-existence between God and humanity, is given in paradigmatic form in "the drama of covenant" between God and Israel. Heschel writes:

> Sinai, the decisive moment in Israel's history, initiated a new relationship between God and man: God became engaged to a people. Israel accepted the new relationship; it became engaged to God. It was an event to which both were partners. God gave His word to Israel, and Israel gave its word of honor to God (p. 214).

As we noticed at the beginning, Heschel finds a description of the third level of his theological exposition in the biblical verse—the people's pledge of commitment at Sinai, "We shall do and we shall hear" (Ex. 24:7).

Strictly speaking, "covenant" is not a unitary term in the Bible. Besides the Mosaic covenant, to which Heschel gives primary attention, there is also the Abrahamic covenant of priestly tradition and the royal covenant with its twin convictions of the divine election of the Davidic king and of Zion as the holy sanctuary. Each of these three covenant patterns of symbolization nuances differently the presence of the Holy God in the world. Heschel apparently leaves it to biblical theologians to consider the various covenants between God and Israel and how the covenant traditions interact with each other. He is concerned basically with a phenomenological description of the relation between God and human beings as seen through the Sinai covenant. Coexistence with God, he maintains, means partnership with God in the redemption of the world. Indeed, every person "is called upon to be a redeemer" (p. 313). Heschel is on sound biblical ground, I believe, when he says that the *imago Dei* of Genesis 1:26–27 is something more than "an analogy of being" as traditionally understood. The role of *'adam*, consisting of "male and female," is to represent God's rule on earth and hence to "image" God through the actions of a vice-regent in the Creator's world and responsible caretaker of the Creator's garden. This is what Heschel calls "an analogy in acts." "It is this likeness of acts—'to walk in His ways'— that is the link," says Heschel, "by which man may come close to God," indeed may imitate God (p. 289).

At this point we come upon one of Heschel's fundamental themes: that God needs human beings. Those who believe with Calvin that the Bible bears witness to God's sovereignty may stumble over these words at first. In what sense does God "need" anything or anyone? Surely God does not suffer from a lack or deficiency. And, granting that God's love does not permit divine solitude, would it not be better to say that God "wants" a relationship with creatures? Doubtless, Heschel would not back down under questioning. He would answer by saying that the need is two-way. Human beings need God, owing to the constitution of their own existence, which impels them to ask the ultimate questions and to stand in radical amazement. And God needs human beings, precisely because God is not part of the world, indeed, is a "stranger" in it. Heschel puts it this way: "God is not indifferent to man's quest for Him. He is in need of man, in need of man's share in redemption. God who created the world is not at home in the world, in its dark alleys of misery, callousness, and defiance" (p. 156).

The matter can be put even more strongly. God needs human witnesses in order to "exist" (be present) in the world. I hear that Heschel liked to quote an ancient rabbinic interpretation of a passage from the prophecy of (Second) Isaiah in which the God of Israel speaks: "You are my witnesses and I am God" (Isa. 43:12–13). This translation, which differs from most modern readings of the text, was boldly interpreted by Rabbi Shimon bar Yohai to mean: "If you are my witnesses, I am God; if you are not my witnesses, it is as if I am not God."[9] It is through human deeds, says Heschel, that God becomes present in the world as the God who cares, the God of pathos. "God is hiding in the world and it is our task to let the divine emerge from our deeds" (p. 358).

Inseparably related to the theology of deed is the anthropology of deed. "To be or not to be"—that is the ontological question for every person. But what does it mean to be—to be this existing one at this time and in this place? Heschel rejects the rationalism of Descartes' "I think, therefore I am," in favor of Joshua's "choose this day whom you will serve" (Josh. 24:15). The stress falls upon the will: decision and responsible action. "The fabulous fact of man's ability to act, *the wonder of doing,*" Heschel says, "is no less amazing than the marvel of being" (p. 285). In fact, "it is in *deeds* that man becomes aware of what his life really is. . . . The heart is revealed in deeds" (p. 284). And when the deed is performed in faith, in response to the divine act, it takes part in the drama of the divine purpose in the world.

In this perspective, the observance of the Torah—now understood in its halachic aspect—is not a mere "religious behaviorism," an empty legalism, at least for the person of faith who identifies with the believing and worshiping community. "Halacha," Heschel writes, "represents the strength to shape one's life according to a fixed pattern; it is a form-giving force" (p. 336). And this strength to shape one's life, to walk with integrity and meaning, is not a human achievement. To quote the well-known words of the psalmist, it is the "fool" who says in his heart (mind) that there is no God and who determines to live according to his own resources and in terms of his own values (Ps. 14:1). The sage, on the other hand, humbly meditates on the Torah and, as we read in Psalm 1, is like a tree planted by living water. The distinction between the foolish and the wise, in the biblical view, is not measured by ignorance versus knowledge. Rather, the difference is the starting point of faith: the "fear [awe] of the Lord" which is the beginning and premise of wisdom. Once again it must be said that the torah-law is dependent on the torah-story of the manifestation of divine "glory" in the world. This "glory" of divine holiness, says Heschel, "manifests itself as a power overwhelming the world." But the divine glory does not merely overwhelm. "Demanding homage, it is a power that descends to guide, to remind" (p. 82). Human beings are not left by themselves to wander in a wilderness; they are given guidance on how they should walk and the direction in which they should go.

There are many questions that would have to be explored further at this point. One has to do with the interpretation of the "law." Clearly, Heschel believes that the "guidance" that God has given in the Torah must be interpreted in the light of post-biblical (Talmudic) tradition. Judaism, he points out, is not purely biblical religion (p. 274). Another question is the degree to which the laws of the Torah are binding upon people today, for Heschel assumes constantly that God's revelation, mediated through Israel, touches human existence itself and therefore has universal implications. And finally, there is the question of human fallibility in the observance of the commandments. Those who suppose, on the basis of past Christian discussions, that the "works of the law" have a questionable, or even negative, value, should read Heschel's discussion of whether "faith alone" is adequate (pp. 293–303). Heschel admits, with true prophetic insight, that all of our actions are tainted with self-will and that any efforts, undertaken in a spirit of self-sufficiency, are bound to end in frustration and failure.[10] This realistic estimate of human action must be seen in the context of God's initiative and purpose as revealed in the Bible. Despite problems on the human side, he writes, this is our hope: "God will redeem where we fail; he will complete what we are trying to achieve. It is the grace of God that helps those who do everything within their power to achieve that which is beyond their power. . . . We must constantly remember: *we spoil and God restores*" (p. 407). In the time given to us, however, we are called to make a "leap into action," for that is what a leap of faith really means. The truth is not to be found by sitting on the sidelines of history as a spectator but, like Abraham, by making a venture. It is through "the ecstasy of deeds" that one may be assured of "the hereness of God," for "right living is a way to right thinking" (p. 283).

The Drama of History

It is difficult to bring this discussion to a conclusion, for Heschel's thought not only commands our attention to major themes of biblical theology but invites us to follow the tributaries that flow into the main currents of biblical tradition. Speaking as a biblical theologian, I find his interpretation of the faith of ancient Israel, as expressed in the literature of the Bible, to be authentic and illuminating.

Though Heschel's starting point in the exposition of biblical theology is the sense of the holy, he places great emphasis upon the Sinai covenant. The God who is revealed as redemptive concern and ethical demand chooses to enter into relationship to a people and to be involved with them in the story of their life. Covenantal relationship with God, however, is strained almost to the breaking point by the terrible sufferings and horrendous evils of history. Heschel is sensitive to, and agonizes over, this theological problem. Across the pages of the book under discussion, *God In Search of Man,* falls the shadow of the Holocaust. The human predicament, he says, has acquired a new gravity and urgency, for we live in "a civilization where factories were established in order to exterminate millions of men, women, and children; where soap was made of human flesh." "What have we done to make such crimes possible?" he asks. "What are we doing to make such crimes impossible?" (p. 369). And his book on *The Prophets,* published a decade later, picks up this question. The book carries a dedication inscribed. "To the martyrs of 1940–45," underneath which is a quotation from Psalm 44, a community lament:

> All this has come upon us,
> Though we have not forgotten Thee,
> Or been false to Thy covenant.
> Our heart has not turned back,
> Nor have our steps departed from Thy way . . .
> . . . for Thy sake we are slain . . .
> Why dost Thou hide Thy face?　　　(Psalm 44:17, 18, 22, 24)

Elie Wiesel, I am told, once asked the literary critic, Alfred Kazin, the question: "Is there an explanation for the Holocaust?" And the answer was: "I hope not." A similar question was asked by the prophet Habakkuk in a time when violence, though less monstrous than the Jewish holocaust, swept like an avalanche over the world and left in its wake a destroyed Jerusalem and a people scattered in exile (Hab. chap. 1). Even within the biblical period, covenantal theology was tried in the balance and found wanting. The sage Job, stunned by a punishment that did not fit the crime, boldly expostulated with God, only to find himself, at the very limit of human thought, confronted by the divine Mystery. And apocalyptic writers, as in the case of the apocalypse of Daniel, perceived that in this present evil age God is hidden. Faith, according to this esoteric view, is strengthened by the revelation of the divine Mystery ("secret") that the God who is now hidden will soon come in power to destroy the forces of evil and to establish the Kingdom of God on earth as it is in heaven.

In our time the problem of evil rears its ugly head in many forms, testing and challenging covenant theology, if not theology itself. In addition to the Jewish holocaust, one thinks of the holocaust of Hiroshima and Nagasaki, of the tragedy of Vietnam, of the unheard cries of human suffering in many places of the world, to say nothing of the threat of an atomic holocaust which hangs precariously, like a Sword of Damocles, over our heads every moment. In such a situation we hear the steady and powerful voice of a distinguished rabbi,

Abraham Joshua Heschel, who speaks out of a tradition that is, as he puts it, "immune to despair." He writes:

> Though events do not run according to a predestined plan, and though the ultimate goal can never be expressed in one word or in words at all, we believe that history as a whole has a meaning that transcends that of its parts. We must remember that God is involved in our doings, that meaning is given not only in the timeless but primarily in the timely, in that task given here and now. Great are man's possibilities. For time is but a little lower than eternity, and history is a drama in which both man and God have a stake. In its happenings we hear the voice as well as the silence of God (pp. 207–8).

In this context, Heschel says that this meaning of history and our historical task is perceived "in the light of the Bible" (p. 206). It is the Bible, the drama of God's search for humanity and of God's engagement with Israel, that captures Heschel's thought, providing him with his basic perspective. Where else can you find such a lofty estimate of the Bible than in the words of praise that run through his whole chapter 25 on "The Bible and the World"? "Other books you can try to account for," he says, "but an attempt to explain the Bible is a supreme opportunity to become ridiculous" (p. 241).

It is precisely Heschel's emphasis on the Bible that makes his thought at once creative and controversial. There are many in the Jewish community who question whether Judaism is indeed a "confrontation with the Bible," for the Talmud has claimed prior attention for many centuries. Moreover, in the Christian community, biblical theology, including the theology of the Old Testament, has been in a state of crisis for some time. Yet we should not miss the creative challenge of Heschel's dramatic view of Scripture, especially in this ecumenical period of interfaith discussion. Three major religions—Judaism, Christianity, and Islam—trace their roots to the Bible, specifically to Abraham the ancestor of faith. How are these three communities, indeed, how is the whole human race related to "the great story and plot of all time and space" and how are we, whoever and wherever we are, related to God, "the Great Dramatist and Storyteller" (to quote the words of Amos Wilder)?[11] This question, when raised by those who are aware of their coexistence and partnership with God in the biblical drama, could evoke awe and wonder at the incomprehensible grace and wisdom of God. So it was in the case of Paul who, after struggling with the interrelation of the Jewish and Christian communities in the economy of God's purpose (Romans 9–11), concluded with an ascription of praise to the God who both transcends and is involved in human history:

> O the depth of the riches and wisdom and knowledge of God!
> How unsearchable are His judgments,
> and how inscrutable His ways!

Paul then quotes twice from the Scriptures of Israel. First from the prophecy of (Second) Isaiah: "For who has known the mind of the Lord, or has been His counselor?" (Isa. 40:13). And second from Job: "Or who has given a gift to Him that He might be repaid?" (Job 35:7).

Such theocentric praise may embrace all those who, with radical amazement, though in diverse perspectives, perceive in faith that—as Heschel put it incisively—"history is a drama in which both God and man have a stake" and in whose "happenings we hear the voice as well as the silence of God."

Notes

1. Abraham J. Heschel, *God In Search of Man: A Philosophy of Judaism* (New York: Farrar, Straus and Cudahy, 1955), p. 25, and see my essay, "Confrontation with the Bible," presented during a memorial "Evening of Tribute," March 4, 1973 at Princeton University, and published in *Theology Today*, 30 (1973), 267–271.
2. "Will Herberg as Biblical Theologian," introduction to the volume of Herberg's essays *Faith Enacted as History: Essays in Biblical Theology* (Philadelphia: Westminster Press, 1976), 9–28. See also my essay on "Will Herberg as Theologian and Philosopher in a Christian Environment," presented at the Drew University Graduate School Colloquium, October 28, 1983, in the forthcoming publication by Fortress Press.
3. See the comments by E. La B. Cherbonnier in his perceptive essay, "A. J. Heschel and the Philosophy of the Bible," *Commentary*, 27 (1959), 23–29, especially p. 27: "The logician alone," Cherbonnier writes, "is not only half a man; he is, according to Heschel, half a philosopher as well. For the truth which the philosopher seeks is better served by beauty and reason together, than by reason alone."
4. Hereafter, the page number(s) placed in parentheses at the end of a quotation will refer to Heschel's book, *God In Search of Man: A Philosophy of Judaism* (New York: Farrar, Straus and Cudahy, 1955).
5. Rudolf Otto, *The Idea of the Holy*, 2nd ed., trans. by John W. Harvey (London: Oxford University Press, 1950).

6. "Theology is like sculpture," writes Heschel in *The Insecurity of Freedom* (New York: Farrar, Straus, and Giroux, 1966) "depth theology is like music. Theology is in the books; depth theology is in the hearts. The former is doctrine, the latter is an event" (p. 36). Quoted and discussed by Byron L. Sherwin in *Abraham Joshua Heschel*, from the Makers of Contemporary Theology series (Atlanta: John Knox Press, 1979), pp. 20–22.

7. See also the illuminating essay by Fritz A. Rothschild, "Truth and Metaphor in the Bible," *Conservative Judaism*, 25 (1971), 3–22.

8. Emil Fackenheim, *God's Presence in History; Jewish Affirmations and Philosophical Reflections* (New York: New York University Press, 1970). See also Martin Buber, *Moses: The Revelation and the Covenant* (New York: Harper and Bros., 1958), pp. 75–77.

9. See Byron L. Sherwin, *op. cit.*, 38.

10. See Will Herberg's perceptive review of Heschel's *God In Search of Man* in *The Christian Century* (April 18, 1956), p. 486.

11. Amos Wilder, *The Language of the Gospel* (New York: Harper and Row, 1964), 64–65.

5

Heschel's Theology of Divine Pathos

JOHN C. MERKLE

It is now more than half a century since the completion and defense of Abraham Heschel's doctoral dissertation. Submitted to the Department of Philosophy at the University of Berlin in 1933, Heschel's dissertation, *Die Prophetie*,[1] is an analysis of prophetic consciousness from the standpoint of comparative religion and from literary, phenomenological, and theological perspectives. Its principal thesis is not simply original but indeed revolutionary; it is the controversial doctrine of divine pathos. Nearly three decades later, in 1962, this same doctrine was elaborated in English in a much more comprehensive book, *The Prophets*.[2]

The purpose of this essay is to summarize, analyze, and interpret Heschel's theology of pathos and to defend it against the most sustained and, to this date, virtually unanswered criticism it has received—that advanced by Eliezer Berkovitz 2 years after the publication of *The Prophets*.[3]

The Pathos of Divine Concern

In Heschel's view, the idea of divine pathos is "*the* central idea in prophetic theology" and "is an explication of the idea of God In Search of Man" which is "the summary of Jewish theology."[4]

The phrase "God in search of man" suggests God's care or concern for human beings. And, according to Heschel, concern for others—what he calls transitive concern—implies pathos, being moved or affected by others. God, whose transitive concern is infinite, is intimately affected by objects of divine concern, particularly by human beings. Heschel explains:

> To the prophet . . . God does not reveal himself in an abstract absoluteness, but in a personal and intimate relation to the world. He does not simply command and expect obedience; He is also moved and affected by what happens in the world, and reacts accordingly. . . . Quite obviously in the biblical view, man's deeds may move Him, affect Him, grieve Him or, on the other hand, gladden and please Him. This notion that God can be intimately affected, that He possesses not merely intelligence and will, but also pathos, basically defines the prophetic consciousness of God.[5]

There are different degrees of transitive concern. To be concerned for the welfare of persons does not always signify "a personal and intimate relation" to them. The kind of concern that signifies such a relation is "a feeling of intimate concern," and it is this type of concern, says Heschel, that God has for human beings. "He is a lover engaged to His people, not only a king. God stands in a passionate relationship to man."[6] To have a passionate relationship with human beings is not only to be concerned for their welfare, but to be moved and affected by their deeds and their plight. Being passionately involved with human beings, God is concerned to the point of being stirred by their doings and by the conditions in which they dwell.

The very fact that human beings are historical creatures means that God's involvement with them must be historical, entailing a dynamic relationship in which there is call and response on both sides. Since God is truly involved in the lives of human beings, God relates to them according to where they are and what they are feeling, thinking, willing, and doing. This means that the attitudes and actions of God vis-a-vis human beings are subject to change, as humans change in relation to God, each other, and the world. God's loving concern for human beings is eternal, but the expressions of that concern are historical, otherwise they would not signify God's involvement with historical beings. Thus it is that "whatever man does affects not only his own life, but also the life of God insofar as it is directed to man."[7] And this is so even to the point of suffering.

Divine Suffering

"God does not stand outside the range of human suffering and sorrow. He is personally involved in, even stirred by, the conduct and fate of man."[8] History is often the record of human misery; and since God is concerned for human beings and involved in their history, God must be involved in their suffering. "God's participation in human history . . . finds its deepest expression in the fact that God can actually suffer."[9]

The anguish of God echoes throughout the Bible. By way of example, Heschel comments on Isaiah 42:14: "The allusion to the Lord as 'a woman in travail,' the boldest figure used by any prophet, conveys not only the sense of supreme urgency of His action, but also a sense of the deep intensity of His suffering." Heschel also reminds us that "of God's involvement in human suffering the prophet declares courageously: '*In all their affliction He was afflicted*'" (Isaiah 63:9).[10]

Heschel would indeed concur with Whitehead's famous comment: "God is the great companion—the fellow-sufferer who understands."[11] Pathos is concern unto suffering. And God's concern is full of pathos.

Pathos, Passion, and Ethos

In Heschel's view, care or concern is the essence of life. But there are different kinds of concern that constitute life. Heschel makes a distinction between reflexive concern, which is directed toward self, and transitive concern, which is directed toward others.[12] As God's concern is transitive, so too is the pathos of that concern.[13] The passion of reflexive concern is self-centered; the pathos of transitive concern is other-directed. God's pathos is realized in response to, and for the sake of, human beings.

As an expression of transitive concern, the pathos of God, though itself a form of passion, is unlike the passions of the pagan gods.

> The pagan gods had animal passions, carnal desires, they were more fitful, more licentious than men; the God of Israel has a passion for righteousness. The pagan gods had selfish needs, while the God of Israel is only in need of man's integrity. The need of Moloch was the death of man, the need of the Lord is the life of man.[14]

The fact that God's pathos is "a passion for righteousness" means that the divine pathos, though an emotional response, is "understood not as an unreasoned emotion, but as an act formed with intention, depending on free will, the result of decision and determination."[15] Acts of passion can be "devoid of reasoned purpose" but they need not be; "emotion can be reasonable just as reason can be emotional."[16] The divine pathos is divine reason and will charged with passion; or it is God's passion informed by reason and will. As such, it is not a blind or uncontrolled reaction that operates automatically but a free response made intentionally.

Another implication of the fact that God's pathos is "a passion for righteousness" is that "ethos is inherent in pathos":

> There is no dichotomy of pathos and ethos, of motive and norm. They do not exist side by side, opposing each other; they involve and presuppose each other. It is because God is the source of justice that His pathos is ethical; and it is because God is absolutely personal—devoid of anything impersonal—that His ethos is full of pathos. Pathos, then, is not an attitude taken arbitrarily. Its inner law is the moral law.[17]

The fact that the inner law of pathos is the moral law does not mean that its inner law is a matter of "strict justice." God's pathos never disregards the standards of justice, but, as compassion and forgiveness, it transcends justice alone. "When the people seem to be doomed by their own deeds, the mercy and grace of God may save them from disaster. Divine pathos may explain why justice is not meted out in the world."[18] In the biblical tradition, injustice is condemned, strict justice is surpassed.

Pathos and Ontology

Heschel's idea of divine pathos is directly opposed to the classical Jewish and Christian metaphysical theology inspired by Greek philosophy. Yet he believes this idea accords with the biblical understanding of God and renders a more accurate interpretation of the theology implicit in the piety of the Jewish tradition than does the classical doctrine of God's impassibility.

It is because of its being steeped in Greek philosophical presuppositions that classical metaphysical theology opposes the idea of divine pathos. These Greek presuppositions are both ontological and psychological. "The static idea of divinity is the outcome of two strands of thought: the ontological notion of stability and the psychological view of the emotions as disturbances of the soul."[19] Heschel examines each of these Greek strands of thought, shows their incompatibility with the biblical understanding of God, and advances the doctrine of pathos as "a more plausible view of ultimate reality."[20]

Concerning ontology, Heschel points to the formidable influence of Parmenides on later philosophical theology. According to Parmenides, being is immovable; movement illusory. Although later Greek philosophy recognized the reality of change, as stressed by Heraclitus, it tended to restrict Heraclitus' theory to the world of sense perception. Classical metaphysical theology applied Parmenides' concept of unchangeable being to God, affirming the Greek assumption that change implies an imperfection that is incompatible with the divine being. Heschel responds to the ontology of Parmenides' Eleatic school and to the metaphysical theology based thereupon as follows:

> The Eleatic premise that true being is unchangeable and that change implies corruption is valid only in regard to being as reflected in the mind. Being in reality, being as we encounter it, implies movement. If we think of being as something beyond and detached from beings, we may well arrive at an Eleatic notion. An ontology, however, concerned with being as involved in all beings or as the source of all beings, will find it impossible to separate being from action or movement, and thus postulate a dynamic concept of divine Being. . . .
>
> Biblical ontology does not separate being from doing. What *is*, acts. The God of Israel is a God who acts, a God of mighty deeds. The Bible does not say how He is, but how He acts. It speaks of His acts of pathos and of His acts in history; it is not as "true

being" that God is conceived, but as the *semper agens*. Here the basic category is action rather than immobility. Movement, creation of nature, acts within history rather than absolute transcendence and detachment from the events of history, are the attributes of the Supreme Being.[21]

The fact that Heschel ascribes mobility or movement to God sets him apart from classical philosophical theology. Yet the fact that he claims that God is moved by non-divine reality sets him even further apart from such classical thought. "Here the basic category is action rather than immobility," and some of God's actions come in the form of reactions, responses to human actions. Not only is God self-moving, acting in relation to the world; God is also moved by other selves, reacting in relation to the world. This, precisely, is the meaning of divine pathos. "The divine pathos which the prophets tried to express in many ways was not a name for His essence but rather for the modes of His reaction to Israel's conduct which would change if Israel modified its ways."[22] Whether God is viewed as self-moving in relation to the world or as moved by beings in the world, in either case God is quite unlike the Unmoved Mover of classical theism. The God of Israel, in Fritz Rothschild's apt description, is "the Most Moved Mover."[23]

The fact that God is moved, or in movement, implies that there is "history in God,"[24] that God is somehow mutable. But does this mean that God, in essence, changes? Recall that Heschel says "the divine pathos . . . was not a name for His essence." He also claims "the divine pathos is not conceived of as an essential attribute of God . . . , but as an expression of God's will."[25] In other words, "a subject of pathos, God Himself is not pathos."[26] Yet a subject of pathos must be a passible subject (i.e., a subject capable of being affected, able to feel and suffer, and thereby to experience change). Pathos may not be "an essential attribute of God," but Heschel would have to admit that passibility is. For pathos is only possible in a being that is in essence passible.

But this does not mean that the divine essence is changeable. The fact that God's modes of reacting to the world are mutable does not mean that God changes in essence. To be, in essence, possible is not the same as to have a possible essence. To be, in essence, possible is to be by nature a being who may change modes of action and reaction; to have a passible essence is to have a changing nature—for example, now human, now divine, or now living, now inanimate. God's nature may be immutable while the modes of God's being-in-relation may change. Specifically, while God *is* the transcendent, transitive concern for being,[27] the expressions of that concern are historical and subject to change.

One reason that classical theism refuses to acknowledge divine change is that God is viewed as perfect, and change is thought to imply imperfection. Why change, so it is thought, unless one's present state of being is less than perfect? According to the philosophic definition of perfection as pure actuality, it must be admitted that a passible God is not perfect, for such a God has not yet actualized all the expressions of divine concern that await realization. Yet the Bible is not concerned with that kind of perfection.[28] From a biblical perspective, pure actuality is no synonym for divine perfection; God suffers change not because of any imperfection but because different situations demand different divine replies. Nowhere does Heschel suggest that God changes for the better. Divine mutability need not imply that God is in the process of becoming more divine. If God is passible, it is because there is potential in God: the potential to be affected and to enact responses not yet actual. But this does not mean that God is thereby perfected.

While it may be a humble confession of faith to speak of the divine response to human outcry, it would be insolence, at least from a perspective such as Heschel's, to suggest that God evolves or develops as a result of the divine-human encounter. We may move God because God allows us to do so. We need not assume that by doing so we somehow enhance God's divinity. Mutability is no sign of imperfection, just as immutability is no sign of perfection. There is history in God not because of a divine imperfection but because God is perfectly responsive to the vicissitudes of history.

Pathos and Psychology

It is the acceptance not only of a Greek ontological presupposition but also of a Greek psychological presupposition that has caused classical theism to reject the idea of divine pathos. Classical theists such as Maimonides or Thomas Aquinas, unlike Aristotle from whom they derive philosophical inspiration, do not deny God's concern for creation. They simply deny that God is concerned to the point of being affected by creation. Yet to have concern for human beings while remaining unaffected by their actions, unmoved by their plight, would be to have a rather remote-like concern, if concern at all it be. Whatever can be said of such an attitude, it does not signify the existence of a genuine relationship. But, as we have seen, according to Heschel's interpretation of the biblical testimony, the concern of God is "a feeling of intimate concern" because "God stands in a passionate relationship to man."[29]

Just as the Greek philosophy adopted by classical theism regards change as an imperfection, so does it consider passion or pathos, an affection implying change, as a sign of weakness. Self-sufficiency is a presupposed ideal of such a philosophy and "the dignity of man was seen in the activity of the mind, in acts of self-determination."[30] Since pathos is aroused by something outside the self, and since it is considered to be an emotional reaction rather than an intellectual act, it is viewed as an imperfection. This could only be so, of course, in a philosophical system wherein "reason is dissociated from the emotional life and sharply contrasted with it."[31] It was such dissociation of reason from emotion—for some philosophers, rooted in the supposed bifurcation of soul and body or in the compartmentalization of the soul—and, moreover, "it was such preference [for reason] that enabled Greek philosophy to exclude all emotion from the nature of the Deity, while at the same time ascribing thought and contemplation to it."[32]

> The perfect example of an impassive deity is the God of Aristotle. By identifying the Deity with the First Cause, with something which, while it has the capacity of moving all things, is itself unmoved, Aristotle's Deity has no pathos, no needs. Ever resting in itself, its only activity is thinking, and its thinking is thinking of thinking. Indifferent to all things, it does not care to contemplate anything but itself. Things long for it and thus are set in motion, yet they are left to themselves.[33]

To the extent that Jewish and Christian theologians accept this Greek presupposition as a basis for understanding the meaning of God, to that extent "*apathēs to theion* becomes a fundamental principle in the doctrine of God for both Jewish and Christian theologians."[34]

In genuine Hebraic thinking, however, self-sufficiency, in the sense of the self being unaffected or unmoved by realities outside the self, is no ideal.[35] Moreover, the dissociation of reason from emotion, like the bifurcation of body and soul or the compartmentalization of the soul, is alien to biblical thinking.

The Bible knows neither the dichotomy of the body and soul nor the trichotomy of body, soul, and spirit, nor the trichotomy within the soul. It sets up no hierarchy in the inner life, nor does it tend to compartmentalize the soul. The heart, regarded as "the totality of the soul as a character and operating function," is the seal of all inner functions, of knowledge as well as of emotion. To put it in different terms: the mind is not a member apart, but is itself transformed into passion.[36]

It follows, then, that "there is no disparagement of emotion, no celebration of apathy" in the biblical perspective. "It is as nonbiblical to separate emotion or passion from spirit as it is to disparage emotion or passion." In fact, says Heschel, "thought is part of emotion. We think because we are moved. . . . Emotion may be defined as the consciousness of being moved." This is why, as we have seen, "emotion can be reasonable, just as reason can be emotional." And not only is emotion or passion important to the life of reason, it is also indispensable to the life of action: "Great deeds are done by those who are filled with *ruaḥ*, with pathos."[37]

Given this positive appreciation of emotion, passion, or pathos in the Bible, "there was no reason to shun the idea of pathos in the understanding of God."[38] In fact, Heschel suggests that an apathetic God would be irrelevant to human beings for whom "the supreme issue is not the question whether in the infinite darkness there is a ground of being which is an object of man's ultimate concern, but whether the reality of God confronts us with a pathos."[39] And not only is divine pathos the supreme issue; it has also been, as we have seen, a privileged or supreme experience in the biblical tradition. Therefore, "to the biblical mind the conception of God as detached and unemotional is totally alien."[40]

Heschel's contrast between the apathetic God of classical theism and the biblical God of pathos is perhaps best summarized in the following excerpt:

An apathetic and ascetic God would have struck biblical man with a sense, not of dignity and grandeur, but rather of poverty and emptiness. Only through arbitrary allegorizing was later religious philosophy able to find an apathetic God in the Bible.

Impressive as is the thought that God is too sublime to be affected by events on this insignificant planet, it stems from a line of reasoning about a God derived from abstraction. A God of abstraction is a high and mighty First Cause, which, dwelling in the lonely splendor of eternity, will never be open to human prayer; and to be affected by anything which it has itself caused to come into being would be beneath the dignity of an abstract God. This is a dogmatic sort of dignity, insisting upon pride rather than love, upon decorum rather than mercy.

In contrast with the *primum movens immobile*, the God of the prophets cares for His creatures, and His thoughts are about the world. He is involved in human history and is affected by human acts.[41]

It is clear that Heschel regards the idea of divine pathos as not only religiously important but philosophically credible, superior to the idea of divine impassibility and apathy. A God unaffected by human concerns, unmoved by human cries, would be religiously irrelevant to human beings and both ontologically and psychologically inferior to those same beings who themselves are able to respond to the concerns and cries of their fellows. What in this regard human beings may do humanly, the God of Israel does divinely, supremely. Such a God alone is God.

Critique of Heschel's Theology of Pathos

It is in his theology of divine pathos that, as Fritz Rothschild rightly claims, "Heschel has propounded a truly revolutionary doctrine, challenging the whole venerable tradition of Jewish and Christian metaphysical theology from Philo, Maimonides, and Thomas Aquinas to Herman Cohen, Étienne Gilson, and Paul Tillich."[42] It is to be expected, then, that Heschel's theology of pathos would be attacked by other theologians. Chief among these critics is Eliezer Berkovits, whose rebuttal appeared soon after Heschel's theology of pathos was expounded in *The Prophets*. The essence of Berkovits' criticism is this: The theology of pathos presupposes an analogy between the divine and the human which is an alien and objectionable concept from the Jewish point of view; thus, a God of pathos "is a God shaped in the image of man."[43] Berkovits claims that Heschel's affirmation of divine pathos is based on a fallacious line of deductive reasoning and on a literalist interpretation of biblical texts.

Concerning Heschel's line of reasoning, Berkovits says:

The logical deduction runs like this: According to the Bible, the greatness of God is seen in the fact that "man is not an abstraction to Him, nor His judgment a generalization." God knows man, the individual human being, and judges Him as an individual. "Yet in order to realize a human being not as a generality but as a concrete fact, one must feel him, one must become aware of him emotionally." This would make sense if God's pathos could be explained logically. But since what we gain by the argument must be called a mystery, why don't we call for a mystery a step sooner? Why not reason in the following manner: It is inconceivable that the Supreme Being should be passible. Therefore, there could be no such thing as divine pathos. At the same time, God realizes man as "a concrete fact." However, in order to do that, one must feel him, one must become aware of him emotionally. But God is free of pathos. Ergo, God's realizing man as a concrete fact and not as an abstraction is enrapt in mystery. We believe our way of reasoning is much more valid than that of Heschel. For Dr. Heschel commits the unforgivable fallacy that he equates the human way of realizing a fellow man as a concrete fact with the way of God. Man's way of "knowing" a fellow being depends on feeling and emotion. Could not conceivably God's way be different from that of man? Surely, our mystery is much more logical than Dr. Heschel's.[44]

Is Berkovits' way of reasoning really "much more valid than that of Heschel"? Is his mystery really "much more logical than Dr. Heschel's"? Is it really logical at all to suggest, as Berkovits does, that God is impassible yet involved in a relationship with historical beings wherein they are realized as concrete facts of history? How can God "realize" concrete human beings while remaining unmoved by them? How can God be concerned with humans in any intimate sense and remain unaffected by human concerns? On the other hand, is it really illogical for Heschel to suggest that God is passible and concerned, yet supreme?

The issue gets down to the starting points for both Heschel and Berkovits. Berkovits begins with the preconceived notion that God is impassible: "Why not reason in the following manner: It is inconceivable that the Supreme Being should be passible. . . ." Heschel begins not with a preconceived notion but with an observation concerning biblical faith: "It is the greatness of God according to the Bible that man is not an abstraction to Him, nor is His judgment a generalization."[45] Berkovits starts with the presupposition that God is absolutely different, "totally other," and hence impassible. Heschel starts with the divine-human relationship in which it is evident, according to a biblical perspective, that God is supreme but not the absolute antithesis of humanity. While Berkovits claims that the analogy between the divine and the human and the consequent belief in God's pathos are "from the Jewish point of view . . . alien and objectionable concepts,"[46] Heschel claims just the opposite: "The Wholly Other is the sharp antithesis to the consciousness of man" and "absolute antithesis is alien to the Hebrew mind."[47] Thus, for Heschel, "the fact that the attitudes of man may affect the life of God, that God stands in an intimate relationship to the world," an observation of Jewish faith, "implies a certain analogy between Creator and creature."[48] Yet the fact that Heschel affirms an analogy between the divine and the human does not mean, as Berkovits suggests, that the God of pathos "is a God shaped in the image of man." It means, rather, that human beings are shaped in the image of God, a very biblical and Jewish idea indeed. It is therefore wrong for Berkovits to claim that Judaism knows no analogy between the divine and the human. On the contrary, this analogy is central to Judaism.

Because Heschel begins with an observation of Jewish faith, not with a preconceived philosophical notion, he does not have the same dilemma as Berkovits: how to reconcile the notion of God's absolute otherness with the biblical testimony of God's relationship to historical human beings. Heschel must simply point out that there is no incongruity between being the supreme Lord of creation and history while at the same time being intimately related to created beings immersed in history. In fact, from Heschel's perspective, a being unrelated to historical creatures could not qualify as the supreme Lord of creation and history.

Is it not more philosophically consistent, "more logical," to speak of God as both supreme Lord of history and also concerned for, and moved by, historical beings than it is to claim that God is impassible yet in relation to historical beings? And is it not philosophically more cogent to speak of God as the Supreme Lord rather than the Wholly Other if indeed it is true that human beings may encounter God? "If the soul is capable of listening [to God], then it cannot be maintained that there is an infinite, qualitative difference between God and man."[49] And is it not philosophically more tenable to suggest that the Supreme Being supremely realizes the spiritual qualities of creatures than to assume that the Supreme Being is devoid of such qualities? For Heschel, God is supreme, not absolutely different; therefore, God may realize pathos in a supreme way rather than be devoid of it simply because it is an emotion that human beings realize in their own creaturely ways.

This brings us to the question of Heschel's interpretation of biblical texts that suggest emotion or pathos in God. Berkovits claims that Heschel's idea of divine pathos stems in part from the literalist interpretation of biblical texts that ascribe emotions to God.[50] But Heschel himself rejects a strictly literalist interpretation of scripture.[51] It is clear, however, in reading both Heschel and Berkovits that each has a different understanding of literalism. For Heschel, literalism with regard to texts about God means taking the texts as adequate descriptions or renderings of the way God is and acts. For Berkovits, literalism means interpreting the texts about God's being and acting in ways analogous to those of human beings. Thus, for Heschel, anthropomorphic expressions about God need not suggest anthropomorphic conceptions of God, as long as the expressions are not thought of as really depicting God. But for Berkovits, anthropomorphic expressions suggest anthropomorphic conceptions even if the expressions are only thought to reveal an analogy between the divine and the human. In rejecting the literalist interpretation, Heschel means that the words used to speak of God or the actions of God are used indicatively and analogously, not descriptively as if rendering a picture of the way God really is and acts. But when Berkovits rejects the literalist approach, he means to discard even the suggestion that words about God, particularly about the emotions of God, may be understood as indicating an analogy between the human and the divine. Thus, Berkovits rejects Heschel's approach as literalist.

Since Heschel is willing to ascribe emotions to God, Berkovits wonders "how come he does not equip the Almighty with a body too"? Says Berkovits: "The anthropomorphic references to God in the Bible are hardly less conspicuous than the anthropopathetic expressions. Using Dr. Heschel's own method of reasoning, it should not be difficult to prove that God has a body."[52] What Berkovits fails to realize is that, according to Heschel, emotions are not incompatible with the divine since "movements of feeling are no less spiritual than acts of thought" and that "one of the chief uses of the word *ruah* is to denote pathos, passion, or emotion—the state of the soul."[53] It does not follow that just because God shares pathos of spirit with human beings that God might also have a body as do humans. The fact that God and humans have certain attributes in common does not mean that they need have all attributes in common, and Heschel is careful in suggesting just what attributes may be ascribed to both. Passibility, the capacity for pathos, is an attribute that God shares with human beings, though God's pathos is divinely superior.

Berkovits recognizes the fact that "in Dr. Heschel's presentation, God's pathos is much more sublime than that of man," but he rejects Heschel's presentation because the difference between the divine pathos and human pathos "is only one of degree . . . and not of kind."[54] Heschel would probably say that the difference in degree is so great that that makes it a difference in kind, but not such a difference in kind that the two have nothing in common. For Heschel, God and humans are different kinds of beings who, nevertheless, have being, and certain attributes of being, in common.

The belief that God and human beings have certain attributes in common is not anthropomorphism, which is the belief that God is endowed with human attributes. God and humans may both realize the attribute of love, for example, but God does so divinely and humans do so humanly. Yet the same word, love, may be used with regard to both God and human beings. So it is with the attribute of passibility and the act of pathos. God and humans both may realize pathos but not in the same way. "What Isaiah (55:8f) said concerning the thoughts of God may equally apply to His pathos: For My pathos is not your pathos, neither are your ways My ways, says the Lord."[55] The language of pathos may be anthropomorphic or, more precisely, anthropopathetic, but God or the pathos of God is not thought of, at least by Heschel, as anthropomorphic or anthropopathetic. "The prophets had to use anthropomorphic language in order to convey His non-anthropomorphic Being."[56] In Heschel's view, God is not conceived anthropomorphically; human beings are understood theomorphically.

According to Berkovits, Heschel's "declaring that God is not anthropomorph but man, theomorph, . . . is of little use" since "a god-like man still implies a man-like god."[57] Berkovits should be reminded that the starting point makes all the difference. A "god-like man," a person who walks in the ways of the Lord, is a biblical concept—"You shall be holy for I the Lord your God am holy" (Lev. 19:2)—and does not imply a human being who is God's equal or replica but one who is God's witness. But a "man-like god" is a pagan concept and implies a being who is not much more than human and deserves not the witness and worship of human beings. Heschel himself is careful to point out the difference between a "god-like man" and a "man-like god": "The likeness of God [in man] means the likeness of Him who is unlike man."[58] Human beings are like God insofar as they give witness to the holiness of God. God is unlike them, however, inasmuch as God is always holy, whereas human beings often defile the holiness with which they have been blessed by God. To speak of a human person who walks in the ways of the Lord is radically different than speaking of a god who walks in human ways, since the ways of humanity are often more demonic than divine. No, a "god-like man" does not imply a "man-like god." The idea of a "god-like man" implies a God whose holiness is such as to warrant witness and whose concern is such as to fill human beings with the qualities that enable them to live in accord with the holiness of God.

One thing remains to be said about whether Heschel takes the biblical texts about God's pathos literally. There is a sense in which he does: Heschel believes that God literally loves and cares for human beings—to the point of being moved by them. That is to say, God is really involved with humans. But this does not mean that Heschel thinks the biblical texts render a literal depiction of the quality and extent of God's love, care, and involvement. "The words of scripture," says Heschel, "are neither identical with, nor the eternally adequate rendering of, the divine wisdom,"[59] nor, by implication, of anything divine. Concerning words used to speak of God and the pathos of God, Heschel writes:

> It is precisely the challenge involved in using inadequate words that drives the mind beyond all words. Any pretension to adequacy would be specious and a delusion. . . .
> *All expressions of pathos are attempts to set forth God's aliveness.* One must not forget that all our utterances about Him are woefully inadequate. But when taken to be allusions rather than descriptions, understatements rather than adequate accounts, they are aids in evoking our sense of His realness.[60]

Berkovits and other classical theists who champion the impassibility of God contend that in this regard God is exactly opposite of what the Bible suggests by its testimony to divine pathos. Heschel would contend that God is greater than, but not contrary to, what the Bible suggests. So while not a strict literalist, Heschel, with his theology of divine pathos, is more faithful to the biblical view of God than is Berkovits and the theological tradition he represents.

Divine Pathos and Human Faith

It is because of God's pathos for human beings that humans are moved to put their faith in God. If God ignored the outcry of human beings, it would be strange indeed for them to cry out to God in faith.

A god who was unmoved by human plight and human deeds would not deserve the faith of beings who themselves are moved by other selves. Only a God who takes human beings seriously is worthy of their faith. And humans are taken seriously only if related to historically. Only a God who responds to human beings deserves their faith. And to respond to them is to be moved by their sufferings and joys, their dreams and deeds.

In short, only a God of pathos is worthy of the faith of human beings who themselves may express pathos for God. It is precisely because God is filled with pathos for human beings that they may respond with sympathy for God. According to Heschel, "the prophet may be characterized as a *homo sympathetikos*," as a person who has "sympathetic solidarity with God" as a result of being "moved by the pathos of God."[61] Prophetic faith is the sympathetic response to divine pathos. And since biblical faith may be characterized as "faith with the prophets,"[62] the revelation of divine pathos is one of the sources of biblical faith. This is why the God of pathos, rather than any impassible god, must be viewed as the primary focus of the biblical tradition.

Notes

1. Abraham Joshua Heschel, *Die Prophetie* (Cracow: The Polish Academy of Sciences, 1936).
2. Abraham Joshua Heschel, *The Prophets* (New York: Harper and Row, 1962). Hereafter cited as *Prophets*.
3. Eliezer Berkovitz, "Dr. A. J. Heschel's Theology of Pathos," *Tradition: A Journal of Orthodox Thought*, 6 (Spring–Summer, 1964), 67–104. Hereafter cited as Berkovits.
4. Abraham Joshua Heschel, "Teaching Jewish Theology in the Solomon Schecter Day School," *The Synagogue School*, 28 (Fall 1969), 4–33, p. 12.
5. *Prophets*, pp. 223–224.
6. Abraham Joshua Heschel, *Man Is Not Alone: A Philosophy of Religion* (New York: Farrar, Straus, and Young, 1951), p. 244. Hereafter cited as *Not Alone*.
7. *Prophets*, p. 226.
8. *Ibid.*, p. 224.
9. *Ibid.*, p. 259.
10. *Ibid.*, p. 151.
11. Alfred North Whitehead, *Process and Reality: An Essay in Cosmology* (New York: The Macmillan Co., 1929), p. 532.
12. Cf. *Not Alone*, pp. 136–139.
13. Cf. *Prophets*, pp. 225–226.

14. *Not Alone*, p. 245.

15. *Prophets*, p. 224.

16. *Ibid.*, p. 256.

17. *Ibid.*, p. 225.

18. *Ibid.*, p. 237.

19. *Ibid.*, p. 260.

20. *Ibid.*, p. 247.

21. *Ibid.*, pp. 262, 264. Again we may note a parallel between Heschel's thought and that of Alfred North Whitehead, the patriarch of modern process philosophy. Although Heschel never addresses the question of an affinity between process philosophy and his own biblical philosophy, it seems clear from the above that, whatever differences there may be between the two, Heschel would be able to concur with one of Whitehead's central tenets: "God is not to be treated as an exception to all metaphysical principles, invoked to save their collapse. He is their chief exemplification." (*Process and Reality*, p. 521.)

22. *Not Alone*, p. 245.

23. Fritz A. Rothschild, ed., *Between God and Man: An Interpretation of Judaism From the Writings of Abraham J. Heschel*, rev. ed. (New York: The Free Press, 1975), p. 25 (cf. next chapter, p. 89).

24. *Prophets*, p. 277.

25. *Ibid.*, p. 231.

26. *Ibid.*, p. 485.

27. Cf., e.g., *Who Is Man?*, pp. 91–92.

28. Cf. *Not Alone*, pp. 101–102, where Heschel points out that the Bible does not speculate about divine perfection. He would agree that the Bible implies God's moral perfection, but that is not the type of perfection being considered presently.

29. *Not Alone*, p. 244.

30. *Prophets*, p. 248.

31. *Ibid.*, p. 250.

32. *Ibid.*

33. *Ibid.*, p. 251.

34. *Ibid.*, p. 254.

35. Within the biblical tradition, the moral ideal is precisely the opposite of the kind of self-sufficiency described above. Edmond La B. Cherbonnier, in "Heschel As A Religious Thinker," *Conservative Judaism*, 23 (Fall 1968), p. 33, points out that this insight of biblical psychology is confirmed by modern psychiatry: "Personal wholeness is also incompatible with another of man's favorite virtues. Man aspires to be self-sufficient, autonomous, invulnerable. But psychiatry provides mounting evidence that the healthy personality is open and vulnerable, willing to take risks and able to bear the hurt. This describes the biblical God *par excellence*. He loves—literally. He feels and cares—literally. This may be Heschel's most significant contribution to religious thought: to emphasize the 'divine pathos,' God's willingness to endure frustration and contempt in His quest for man's response. It is just possible that our resistance to the idea of divine pathos, deeply entrenched in the philosophic tradition,

is in fact a rationalization. It may be motivated by the fear of taking the same risks that God takes. But we shall never be fully human until we give up the rationalization and follow His example."

36. *Prophets*, p. 257.
37. *Ibid.*, pp. 258, 216, 316, 256, 258.
38. *Ibid.*, p. 238.
39. Abraham Joshua Heschel, "The Jewish Notion of God and Christian Renewal," *Renewal of Religious Thought,* Vol. I of *Theology of Renewal,* ed. by L. K. Shook (New York: Herder and Herder, 1968, 105–129, p. 107.
40. *Prophets*, p. 257.
41. *Ibid.,* pp. 258–259.
42. Fritz A. Rothschild, "Architect and Herald of a New Theology," *America,* 128 (March 10, 1973), 210–212, p. 211 (cf. next chapter, p. 88).
43. Berkovits, p. 94; cf. p. 102.
44. *Ibid.*, pp. 81–82.
45. *Prophets*, p. 257.
46. Berkovits, p. 102.
47. *Prophets*, p. 227.
48. *Ibid.*, p. 229.
49. Abraham Joshua Heschel, *A Passion for Truth* (New York: Farrar, Straus and Giroux, 1973), p. 254.
50. Cf. Berkovits, pp. 70, 82–83.
51. Cf., e.g., Abraham Joshua Heschel, *God In Search of Man: A Philosophy of Judaism* (New York: Farrar, Straus and Cudahy, 1955), pp. 178–183. Hereafter cited as *Search*.
52. Berkovits, p. 82.
53. *Prophets*, pp. 259, 315.
54. Berkovits, p. 74.
55. *Prophets*, p. 276.
56. *Ibid.*
57. Berkovits, p. 94.
58. Abraham Joshua Heschel, *The Insecurity of Freedom: Essays on Human Existence* (New York: Schocken Books, 1966), p. 151.
59. *Search*, p. 264.
60. *Prophets*, p. 276–277.
61. *Ibid.*, pp. 308, 313 and 314.
62. *Search*, p. 249.

PART
THREE

*Heschel as
Philosopher and
Poet*

6

Varieties of Heschelian Thought

FRITZ A. ROTHSCHILD

This symposium honors the memory of a great and good man, and those of us who knew him still feel a deep sense of personal loss occasioned by his death. But we also realize that Abraham Joshua Heschel did not leave us empty-handed. This brilliant and productive scholar and thinker bestowed upon us and future generations a rich and many-sided heritage. Not only was Heschel a great man, he was also, I believe, the outstanding Jewish thinker of his generation. I have formed this judgment on the basis of how Heschel satisfied four criteria that may be used to judge the significance of any religious thinker: comprehensiveness, depth, consistency, and relevance.

Four Criteria

Heschel's work exhibits a remarkable range of *comprehensiveness*. It draws on all epochs and aspects of the Jewish tradition. His books and articles deal with biblical theology, ancient rabbinic commentary, medieval philosophy, Jewish mysticism, Hasidic wisdom and piety, and the plight and achievements of modern Jewry. His analysis of prophecy is unsurpassed. And his researches into the problem of revelation and the nature of Torah resulted in an original thesis on two main currents of thought in early rabbinic literature. He has written scholarly works on the metaphysics of the medieval neo-platonic philosopher and poet Ibn Gabirol (Avicebron); on Saadia Gaon, the patriarch of medieval Jewish philosophy; on Maimonides, the greatest philosopher of medieval Jewry; and on Isaac Abravanel, the Jewish statesman and Bible commentator of fifteenth-century Spain. He discovered a hoard of early Hasidic letters and manuscripts, and his subsequent monographs on the history of the Hasidic movement, though not widely known outside the circle of scholars in this subject, have been a major contribution to this little-explored period. But the central theme of Heschel's interest and research was the clarification of the basic problems of religion as they concern contemporary man, and it is in his philosophy of religion that we find his most outstanding and original contribution to the world of letters. In his writings on religion he combines the yearning for holiness and spirituality of his Hasidic ancestors with the yearning for free inquiry and objective truth of the modern Western scholar. Heschel's lifework can thus be seen as consisting of two parallel strands: his studies and interpretations of the classical sources of Judaism, and his endeavor to offer to our generation an authentic religious philosophy, resulting from the application of the insights gained from these classical sources to contemporary problems and perplexities. Heschel, the research scholar, explored the documents of the past in order to make certain that Heschel, the creative thinker, could make his message true and authentic.

Heschel's comprehensive research yielded in him an amazing breadth of vision. Yet his writings are marked even more by *depth* of insight. Heschel's writings penetrate and illumine the reality under-lying religion, the living and dynamic relationship between the divine and the human. Whoever wants truly to come to grips with his basic outlook must read him searchingly. Beneath the *peshaṭ*, the plain sense, one must delve into the "depth theology." The key to Heschel's thought is found in the concept of *personal concern*. The ultimate is not Being, but Concern for being. Few of Heschel's readers are aware that he has propounded a truly revolutionary doctrine, challenging the whole venerable tradition of Jewish and Christian metaphysical theology from Philo, Maimonides, and Thomas Aquinas to Hermann Cohen, Étienne Gilson, and Paul Tillich. He proclaimed that the

Greek categories of "being" and eternally frozen perfection are inadequate to Judaism and must be replaced by a new set of categories derived from biblical thinking. Aristotle's Unmoved Mover must give way to the Bible's Most Moved Mover, the God of pathos who stands in a dynamic and reciprocal relationship to creation (as discussed in the previous chapter by Dr. Merkle).

"Being through creation," through the divine act of freedom, expresses in symbolic form that reality is not a self-sufficient, fixed, mechanical order. It is a process in which human beings may freely react to the challenges of life and in which surprise, novelty, and unexpected creative possibilities always exist. Through sympathy, compassion, and sensitivity to the divine concern, human beings can overcome the egocentric predicament and can fulfill their true potential. The denial of fixed being as the ultimate building block of the universe opens new possibilities for philosophy. The parallel to modern physics, which sees reality as a field of forces rather than a collection of moving billiard balls, is obvious. Future researchers would be well advised to probe the connections and parallels between Heschel's biblical philosophy and process philosophers (e.g., Whitehead, Bergson, and Hartshorne) and existentialists (e.g., Heidegger, Jaspers, and Marcel). In ethics, the idea of concern helps to explain the ideal of care for the fellow creature; in the theory of knowledge, it helps to overcome the paralysis of the cognizing subject locked in the magic circle of Kant's epistemology. In exploring basic human attitudes, it enables us to overcome routine dullness and alienation by reminding us that to be human is to reach beyond ourselves, in *ek-stasis*, transcending our loneliness and isolation in knowledge, action, art, and worship. Space and time take on new meanings in Heschel: Things are merely frozen processes; life itself is a process gathering the past into itself, reaching out into the future. The Sabbath is to Judaism an edifice in time, a cathedral of the spirit. Reality is not like a stone sculpture, but like a symphony.

While it would be difficult to find anyone who would question the depth of Heschel's thought, when it comes to his *consistency* as a thinker we face a problem. His writings exhibit a beauty and vividness of phrase rarely found in scholarly works. The ideas appear in aphoristic flashes of insight, and we may be deceived into the impression that a gifted poet and sage is delighting us with spiritual gems rather than supplying us with a systematic exposition of a coherent philosophy. Like Santayana, the great American philosopher, Heschel's literary artistry makes us forget that the easy-flowing prose hides subtle and complex thought processes that are ours to discover only if we delve beneath the surface and study each passage in depth and in relation to the other passages. Critics have taken exception to what they have called Heschel's euphuistic style, and followers have often merely admired the striking insights of individual passages strung together like pearls on a necklace. Both have overlooked the fact that there is more to Heschel than meets the eye or enchants the soul: that he is a consistent thinker who offers a *Weltanschauung* that can be understood in terms of a set of basic concepts and categories. More than 25 years ago I set myself the task of unearthing the skeleton of Heschel's thought, and it took me a full year before I discerned the basic and consistent pattern underlying his many and diverse ideas. In 1959, my anthology of Heschel's writings, entitled *Between God and Man*, was published. (In 1965, and again in 1975, The Free Press of Macmillan Publishing Company republished this book.) In the book's introduction and by the arrangement of the writings, I attempted to show just how consistent a thinker Heschel was. If my own work does not convince you of Heschel's consistency of thought, may I recommend our symposium director's book, *The Genesis of Faith: The Depth Theology of Abraham Joshua Heschel*, also published by Macmillan. In Professor Merkle's outstanding work, Heschel, who did not write his philosophy in a systematically ordered way, emerges as the consistent thinker he really was.

We have dealt with comprehensiveness, depth, and consistency. What about *relevance?* It is here that Heschel made a truly significant breakthrough in theological method. Writing for his contemporaries, who are perplexed and alienated and for whom old values and formulas have often become meaningless, Heschel is not content just to offer the traditional answers. The first task to him is to recover the questions without which answers are irrelevant. Unless we are concerned with ultimate questions, life becomes flat and meaningless. Heschel's method of correlation, similar to Paul Tillich's but independently conceived, makes the ancient teachings of Judaism relevant by showing that they address themselves to the basic questions of human existence: What is the meaning of my life? How can I attach myself to a reality that can lift me above the dull routine of animal existence? What ought I to do? What may I hope for?

Judaism is a way of life, a discipline of law and observance and a doctrine seemingly confined to a small and peculiar people. Heschel shows how this "scandal of particularity" can be overcome: not by abandoning this ancient faith in favor of a vague broad humanism, but by showing modern Jews that their classical tradition speaks to the concerns of all human beings and is grounded in universal and pervasive traits of our existence. Thus, for example, Judaism teaches that God created the world, revealed the Torah, and will redeem mankind and the world. But to throw these three doctrines at the modern Jew in the style of Karl Barth, like a stone *senkrecht von oben* ("vertically from above"), may hit his skull without penetrating either mind or soul. So instead, Heschel points to experiences through which we can reach God; for example, experiences of nature, of biblical study, and of doing *mitsvot*, sacred deeds.

In our life situation here and now, we can recover the awareness of the holy dimension of existence, the sense of the presence of God and of our relationship to God. By looking at nature, the world we live in, freed from the routine of taking things for granted, we recover the sense of wonder and awe. Far from being a mere subjective mood, this sense of wonder and awe is a basic attitude which enables us to see beyond the mere givenness of data to the ultimate power and ground of all things. Heschel maintains that within all things an indicativeness of what transcends them is given with the same immediacy as the things themselves. We can perceive that indicativeness if we learn to face the grandeur of nature with a sense of wonder and awe. Heschel's writings can help us in this regard: to look afresh at the world of nature, to see in it an allusion to transcendent meaning; to perceive in all created things, especially our fellow human beings, the presence of the divine.

As the world is a pathway to God, so too is the Word. The Bible, read and studied not just as an antiquarian document but as the record of revelation, can again become a voice vibrating across the corridors of time, recalling us to the divine demand, and challenging us to take a stand as responsive and responsible persons. Perhaps more than any author in our time, Heschel helps us perceive life as the biblical prophets and psalmists perceived it; he thereby helps us discern in the biblical message the presence of God.

Finally, by doing *mitsvot* we can experience meanings not available through mere conceptual discourse. Against Kierkegaard's "leap of faith," Heschel declares that Judaism demands a "leap of action," the willingness to learn by doing, to appreciate and to be enriched by an experience that touches the whole person and that goes beyond the mere analysis and reinterpretation of that which we already knew beforehand. In doing sacred deeds, we surpass ourselves and sense the presence of a spirit not our own, we become co-workers in the task of redeeming the world. In his writings, Heschel has shown us how sacred deeds disclose the divine, how by enacting them we become partners of God.

By helping us perceive the divine significance of our human experiences, and by correlating these experiences with principal doctrines and practices of traditional Judaism, Heschel reveals the perennial relevance of a time-honored faith.

Judged by each of the criteria discussed—comprehensiveness, depth, consistency, and relevance—Heschel is clearly an outstanding religious thinker. I know that I am not alone in considering him to be the most significant Jewish religious thinker of our time. Yet, Heschel's thought has stimulated a good deal of controversy and opposition. To this we now turn.

Criticism of Heschel

Heschel's Jewish philosophy has been attacked by two kinds of critics: one thinks that it is not Jewish, the other that it is not philosophy. We can easily dispose of the first type of criticism. It is patently absurd to deny the Jewish character of a thinker who was deeply steeped in all aspects of Judaism, embracing the full richness of the biblical, rabbinic, kabbalistic, and hasidic Jewish tradition. Those critics, who have substituted an anemic, watered-down mixture of modern humanism for the full-bodied and historical tradition that Heschel knew and expounded so well, need not be taken seriously.

But those who maintain that Heschel's religious thought does not represent a philosophy, a reasoned system of arguments of the kind propounded by professional philosophers, seem to have a stronger case (as I indicated earlier when discussing the consistency of Heschel's thought). It is not altogether surprising that some critics have found it useful to dispose of Heschel's thought by calling him a poet rather than a philosopher, thus being able to acknowledge his undoubted brilliance of style, while at the same time avoiding the more difficult task of seriously coming to grips with his arguments. What is ironical and perplexing to me is the fact that not only professed opponents, but also sincere and thoughtful adherents of Heschel have embraced a somewhat similar position. Those who have attacked him have proclaimed that he has failed to give cogent rational arguments for Judaism, and that his work is a lyrical and vivid description of Judaism from the viewpoint of the committed believer, masquerading as a reasoned philosophical proof for the doctrines which he celebrates and advocates. Against these attacks, one outstanding and deeply sympathetic philosopher has defended

Heschel by pointing out that these criticisms are based on a misunderstanding of Heschel's intentions, since the critics "look to him for the performance of one task, when in fact he performs another."[1] Professor Emil Fackenheim makes the helpful distinction between "religious thinking" and "reflective thinking about religion."[2] The former type is based on religious commitment and cannot be expected to provide arguments for religious faith. On the contrary, religious thinking, taking its stand within the theological circle of traditional faith, must inevitably seem to the objective, non-committed outsider to beg the main question. Reflective thinking about religion, on the other hand, is concerned with the task of showing the need and significance of religion in human life and thought. Professor Fackenheim defends Heschel by pointing out that a work such as *God in Search of Man* is engaged in religious thinking and cannot therefore be faulted for lacking persuasive power vis-à-vis the non-committed reader.

Now it seems to me that this interpretation is based on a serious misreading of Heschel's purpose, and it may prevent his readers from understanding some of the most basic intentions of his philosophy of religion and of Judaism.[3] The fact that one of the most lucid and acute Jewish philosophers of our time thus interprets Heschel indicates to me that Heschel himself apparently did not fully succeed in clarifying to his readers the exact nature and methodology of his approach. Since I believe that a clarification of this point will enable others to appreciate better the basic thrust of his philosophy of Judaism, I shall devote the final part of this chapter to an attempt in this direction.

Three Levels of Discourse

Fifteen years ago, I delivered a paper before a convention of rabbis, trying to show that a careful reading of Heschel's works discloses that he *is* a religious philosopher and that he operates on three different levels of discourse.[4] It had the impact of stone thrown into a pond. It created a ripple for about 10 seconds and then sank without a trace. Today I wish to reiterate the arguments of that paper and to illustrate and corroborate my analysis by submitting to you three passages from Heschel's writings, each of which reflects one of these levels of discourse. The fact that Heschel does not state on which of the levels he operates in a given passage, and the additional factor that these levels often overlap or are run together in a single passage, is responsible for many readers' failure to discern these distinct types of discourse and their disparate logical force. Their enumeration, dull as it may be for the reader, is presented in the hope that it will prove a useful methodological tool for understanding Heschel's writings:

LEVEL ONE: EMPIRICAL DESCRIPTION

Since Heschel's philosophy of religion is Jewish, it is important that he use to the fullest the materials of authentic Jewish tradition. This he does in a double-barrelled way. On the one hand, he draws freely upon classical source material ranging from the Bible, the Talmud, the Midrash, and medieval literature through Hasidic teachings and stories. On the other hand, he feels the need to present in vivid colors, to the reader who is a stranger to this type of literature, descriptions of topics which may evoke in him a sympathetic and full-bodied representation. These are the passages that have drawn warm praise from some readers and chilly rejection from others, because they do not argue logically, but present descriptively such subjects as the inner consciousness of the pious Jew at prayer, the experience of Sabbath sanctity, the attitude of wonder and awe in facing nature, and the consciousness of the prophets. Once it is seen that these descriptions do not claim probative force, but are source materials for the historian and analyst of religion, in the way in which case histories are grist for the psychologist's or the social scientist's research, it is possible to appreciate their value and, thus, no longer necessary to deny their legitimacy in the context of religious philosophy.

As an example of level-one discourse, I submit to your consideration this excerpt from Heschel's *Man Is Not Alone:*

The world in which we live is a vast cage within a maze, high as our mind, wide as our power of will, long as our life span. Those who have never reached the rails or seen what is beyond the cage know of no freedom to dream of and are willing to rise and fight for civilizations that come and go and sink into the abyss of oblivion, an abyss which they never fill. . . .

But even those who knocked their heads against the rails of the cage and discovered that life is involved in conflicts which they cannot solve; that the drive of possessiveness, which fills streets, homes, and hearts with its clamor and shrill, is constantly muffled by the irony of time; that constructiveness is staved in by self-destructiveness—even they prefer to live on the sumptuous, dainty diet within the cage rather than look for an exit to the maze in order to search for freedom in the darkness of the undisclosed.

Others, however, who cannot stand it, despair. They have no power to spend on faith any more, no goal to strive for, no strength to seek a goal. But, then, a moment comes like a thunderbolt, in which a flash of the undisclosed rends our dark apathy asunder. It is full of overpowering brilliance, like a point in which all moments of life are focused or a thought which outweighs all thoughts ever conceived of. There is so much light in our cage, in our world, it is as if it were suspended amidst the stars. Apathy turns to splendor unawares. The ineffable has shuddered itself into the soul. It has entered our consciousness like a ray of light passing into a lake. . . .

A tremor seizes our limbs; our nerves are struck, quiver like strings; our whole being bursts into shudders. But then a cry, wrested from our very core, fills the world around us, as if a mountain were suddenly about to place itself in front of us. It is one word: GOD. Not an emotion, a stir within us, but a power, a marvel beyond us, tearing the world apart. The word that means more than universe, more than eternity, holy, holy, holy; we cannot comprehend it. We know it means infinitely more than we are able to echo. Staggered, embarrassed, we stammer and say: He, who is more than all there is, who speaks through the ineffable, whose question is more than our mind can answer; He to whom our life can be the spelling of an answer.[5]

This passage is a highly subjective piece of poetic prose. I think we can confidently assert that here we are dealing with a very intimate testimony based on its author's personal experience. It does not propound a logical argument or a philosophical proposition. In fact, I always thought it was almost exaggeratedly lyrical and somewhat overemotional. It is the merit of Professor Edward Kaplan, in a remarkable paper entitled "Mysticism and Despair in Abraham J. Heschel's Religious Thought," to have pointed out that it is "one of Heschel's literary masterpieces" and that his poetic prose "conveys more than emotional conviction."[6] It contains an almost "Kafkaesque" sense of the absurdity and horror of life. But it also goes on to evoke the experience in which suddenly the horror is changed to wonder, the world which first appeared as a dark cage in which we are held prisoners is now seen as full of light. We live within a cage, but it is "suspended amidst the stars."

This excerpt relates not just a religious or revelational experience, but also contains an evaluation of different types of living and human conduct. Heschel refers to three types of human existence. There are those who accept, or even welcome, life lived within the limits of a purely this-worldly materialistic framework, those who strive to escape the prison of such a meaningless and absurd world, and finally those who have undergone the sudden perception that our life is related to God. These latter realize that mundane reality is not all there is, but that it points to its ultimate source which endows even the seemingly absurd with meaning and splendor. What makes reality a cage and drives us to despair is not the objective reality we face, but our own egocentric predicament. To illustrate my point, let me quote from another passage of Heschel's, because the best comment on an author is usually another passage by that author. Elsewhere in *Man Is Not Alone* Heschel says: "We would rather be prisoners if only our mind, will, passion, and ambitions were the four walls of the prison."[7] This is not just a vivid picture. It is a parable that tells us that we are imprisoned by our own personalities, by the limits of our mind, our will, our passion, and our ambitions. This is not yet philosophy. It does not prove anything, but it describes our human predicament. Yet this is not the whole story of our human situation; there is a way to transcend this predicament, and Heschel describes this well:

> There are moments in which, to use a Talmudic phrase, heaven and earth kiss each other; in which there is a lifting of the veil at the horizon of the known, opening a vision of what is eternal in time. Some of us have at least once experienced the momentous realness of God. Some of us have at least caught a glimpse of the beauty, peace, and power that flow through the souls of those who are devoted to Him. There may come a moment like a thunder in the soul, when man is not only aided, not only guided by God's mysterious hand, but also taught how to aid, how to guide other beings.[8]

This passage is not philosophy as such; it is, rather, a description of an experience that is at the foundation of philosophy; it is the stuff from which philosophical arguments for the credibility of religious faith may be fashioned. It is another example of Heschel's indispensable first level discourse that forms a context for his religious philosophy.

LEVEL TWO: PHENOMENOLOGICAL ANALYSIS

The phenomenological method, advanced by Edmund Husserl whose writings were of decisive influence on Heschel in his student days in Berlin, may briefly be defined as an attempt to present the structures of experienced reality in their essential and archetypal purity. The phenomenologist of religion is not, for example, concerned with the question of whether the God of the prophets really exists, but he is at pains to delineate the structure of the prophets' experience and to elaborate the full categorical framework which explains and clarifies this particular revelatory relationship, without confusing it with accidental features which are not an integral and constitutive part thereof. I think that some of the most solid and enduring achievements of Heschel's work, which have become classics of their kind, are the results of his phenomenological research: his phenomenology of prophetic consciousness which earned him his doctorate; the phenomenological descriptions of the threefold approach to the awareness of God through nature, biblical study, and mitzvot (as treated earlier in this chapter); his phenomenological understanding of the Sabbath experience as sanctification of time; and his typology of prayer. The great achievement of this type of analysis in Heschel's work ought to be appreciated equally by the committed believer and the neutral "objective" non-believer. To the first, it clarifies and illuminates the faith he holds. To the second, it offers a lucid and meaningful picture of Jewish faith in categories which are authentically derived from the experience of that faith *ab intra*, and hence an understanding of Judaism which is not distorted by a categorical framework which has been borrowed from a different universe of discourse. In other words, to the believer, the content of Heschel's book *The Prophets* can offer an understanding of the revelatory events he believes in, while to the historian of religion it can offer an insight into the type of experience which the ancient prophets of Israel claimed to have undergone.

The following quotation from *The Prophets* is an example of level-two discourse:

> Every event is essentially made up of two phases. Since an event is limited in time, it must have a beginning, and since it is not indefinitely continuous, it must run a certain course. The beginning and the course of development together constitute the characteristic structure of every event. The first phase is effected

by a change in the prior, original condition; the second by a
tendency to evolve according to a certain momentum. In the first
phase we have an interruption and ceasing; in the second, a
continuance and progress. The first we term a *turning*, or a
decision; the second, a *direction*. Thus there are two aspects to
inspiration as seen from the prophet's point of view: a moment of
decision, or a turning, and a moment of expression, a direction.

What do we mean by *turning*, or decision?

Every event starts out as a change, as a turning point; a turning
away from a stable condition must take place for the event to
happen. In the change lies the transition from motive to initiative,
the birth of the event out of the motive. . . .

A turning is always pivoted upon the will. The prophets knew
no manifestation of God which was passive, unwilled or unin-
tentional. It was not thought of as proceeding out of God like rays
out of the sun. It was an act proceeding from this will and brought
about a decision to disclose what otherwise would remain
concealed. In this sense, it was an act within the life of God. . . .

What do we mean by *direction?*

A personal event is an act of communication in which an
intention is conveyed to another person. It means addressing a
person. An act of communication has a direction. The turning is
the genesis of the event, the direction its realization. It is a moment
in which an act within a person becomes an act for the sake of
another person. A relationship is established, the event has
reached its end; it has assumed form; it is a maximum of
eventuation. . . .

Revelation is not a voice crying in the wilderness, but an act of
received communication. It is not simply an act of disclosing, but
an act of disclosing *to* someone, the bestowal of a content, God
addressing the prophet. There is no intransitive aimless revelation
in prophecy. God's word is directed to man. . . .

In the light of these structural categories, religious events must
be divided into two types. They are experienced either as a turning
of a transcendent Being toward man, or as a turning of man
toward a transcendent Being. The first may be called *anthro-
potropic*, the second *theotropic*.[9]

In this passage, Heschel carefully distinguishes the prophetic event
from some other kind of religious event, for example, from a mystic
absorption in the deity. Prophecy means that God turns toward
human persons and directs divine activity in relation to them. From

that premise, we are able to work out a whole biblical theology in which the God of the prophets is distinguished, for example, from Aristotle's Unmoved Mover, and biblical religion is distinguished from other types such as those of the Far East.

Whereas the passage containing level-one discourse was an impassioned description of religious experience, this level-two passage is a cool analysis of what constitutes the structure of prophetic experience. Does such level-two discourse contain a philosophy of life or religion? May conclusions about reality be drawn from this passage? Not quite. But when Heschel, as a young student in Berlin, had established these categories in his phenomenology of religion, he laid the foundation of his mature philosophy of life and religion. For if revelation is "an act within the life of God," an event in which God takes the initiative to commune with human persons and to share the divine will and concern with them, then we have a new way of explaining life, ethics, religion, and the meaning of God.

LEVEL THREE: PHILOSOPHICAL APPROACH

Heschel does not stop at the level of phenomenological analysis. He claims that the basic truths and insights revealed in the depiction of Jewish faith are not merely the idiosyncracies of a particular religious outlook. He believes that if sympathetically presented, they will be found relevant to the problems of sensitive men and women beyond the circle of previously committed traditionalists. The endeavor to present this universal aspect of Jewish thought constitutes the main part of his philosophy of religion.

Now it must be stated that Heschel does not believe that Judaism can be demonstrated *more geometrico*. He denigrates the attempts to "prove" the existence of God and would, if I understand him correctly, not claim that he could demonstrate by reason alone the truth of Judaism even to an ideally intelligent and sympathetic reader. But the inability to prove a world outlook or a religious orientation does not mean that such an outlook or orientation must therefore be adopted or rejected on non-rational grounds of blind faith-commitment. In ordinary life we make decisions which are not exclusively motivated by unassailable deductive arguments, but are nevertheless largely supported by rational considerations which have persuasive power. Heschel's philosophy of religion is largely informed by the conviction that the very ideas, values, and attitudes of Judaism which his phenomenological labors have disclosed are not merely the peculiar stance of the tradition of a peculiar people, but are in deepest accord with the values and attitudes of all intelligent and morally sensitive people, once they reflect on these matters and try to gain a perceptive understanding of themselves and the meaning of their lives in the light of the insights gained from the study of Jewish faith.

Thus, for example, Heschel shows that the attitude of wonder and awe disclosed in the biblical approach to nature is a pervasive trait of all openminded human consciousness, and that the same pervasive trait of reality that leads the psalmist to the awareness of God's glory is equally at the root of scientific curiosity and the search for the uniformity of nature and nature's laws. The structure of prophetic responsiveness to the unconditioned demand of God, and sympathetic solidarity with the divine concern, is seen as the archetype of *all* moral response and responsibility. Thus, according to Heschel, even the nominal atheist who recognizes the absolute claim of the moral demand which cannot be reduced to the interests of the self or the interests of society is implicitly recognizing the fact that humanity is answerable to a demand that issues from a transcendent dimension and which is, in traditional language, the Voice of God.

Heschel does not claim to have proved that the only and infallible *Gestalt* of divine revelation, particular legislation, and the modes of worship, celebration, and sanctification are fully embodied in the concrete historical tradition of Judaism. He does, however, claim that nothing significant in human life and our experience of nature and fellow human beings fails to be enhanced in meaning and deepened in understanding and appreciation if viewed through the insights and modes of behavior which we can draw from our religious inheritance.

The following quotation from *Man Is Not Alone* is an example of level-three discourse:

> Together with the potentialities locked up in our nature we possess the key to release and develop them. The key is our aspirations. To attain any value, we must anticipate, seek and crave for it. . . . A person *is* what he aspires for. In order to know myself, I ask: What are the ends I am striving to attain? What are the values I care for most? What are the great yearnings I should like to be moved by? . . .
>
> No code, no law, even the law of God, can set a pattern for all of living. It is not enough to have the right ideas. For the will, not reason, has the executive power in the realm of living. The will is stronger than reason and does not blindly submit to the dictates of rational principles. Reason may force the mind to accept

intellectually its conclusions. Yet what is the power that will make me love to do what I ought to do? . . .

It is natural and common to care for personal and national goals. But is it as natural and common to care for other people's needs or to be concerned with universal ends? Conventional needs like pleasure are easily assimilated by social osmosis. Spiritual needs have to be implanted, cherished, and cultivated by the vision of their ends. . . .

Jewish religious education consists in converting ends into personal needs rather than in converting needs into ends, so that, for example, the end to have regard for other people's lives becomes my concern. Yet, if those ends are not assimilated as needs but remain mere duties, uncongenial to the heart, incumbent but not enjoyed, then there is a state of tension between the self and the task. The perfectly moral act bears a seed within its flower: the sense of objective requiredness within the subjective concern. Thus, justice is good not because we feel the need of it; rather we ought to feel the need of justice because it is good.

Religions may be classified as those of self-satisfaction, of self-annihilation, or of fellowship. In the first, worship is a quest for satisfaction of personal needs like salvation or desire for immortality. In the second, all personal needs are discarded, and man seeks to dedicate his life to God at the price of annihilating all desire, believing that human sacrifice, or at least complete self-denial, is the only true form of worship. The third form of religion, while shunning the idea of considering God a means for attaining personal ends, insists that there is a partnership of God and man, that human needs are God's concern and that divine ends ought to become human needs. . . .

The solution to the problem of needs lies not in fostering a need to end all needs but in fostering a need to calm all other needs. There is a breath of God in every man, a force lying deeper than the stratum of will, and which may be stirred to become an aspiration strong enough to give direction and even to run counter to all winds.[10]

This text, while having its poetic moments (level one), and while presenting a phenomenological description of the relationship between needs and ends (level two), also seeks to persuade its readers of the reasonableness and the universal significance of the Jewish position on the problem described (level three). Heschel suggests that Judaism offers a way to achieve authentic human fulfillment while attending to the needs of our fellow creatures and the dreams of our God. It can help us find "the key to release and develop" the "potentialities locked up in our nature" by implanting in us a vision of spiritual ends, by "fostering a need to calm all other needs," by stirring an "aspiration strong enough to give direction" to life, and by cultivating personal concern for "God's concern." Heschel shows us that Jewish faith is a rational and responsible option because it reveals "a force lying deeper than the stratum of will," the "breath of God in every man" which is "the power that will make me love to do what I ought to do."

We have come full circle. Heschel has shown us that commitment to the ideals of Judaism (and, I am sure he would agree, Christianity) can help us break the bonds of our egocentric predicament and thereby experience the miracle of transcending the limits of our cage. Thus we become aware that we are "suspended amidst the stars."

The philosophical work of a great religious thinker can never replace the need for an existential decision by his readers to make a commitment which involves an element of risk, of faith, and of personal response to their total life situation. But a sensitive reader of Heschel's work will make a decision with deepened insight, a new openness to Jewish tradition, and an awareness of the things that truly matter. There is a distinct possibility that the reader might make a decision in favor of Jewish commitment.

Notes

1. Emil L. Fackenheim, review of *God in Search of Man* by Abraham J. Heschel, *Conservative Judaism* 15 (Fall 1960), p. 50.
2. Ibid.
3. Cf. John C. Merkle's book, *The Genesis of Faith: The Depth Theology of Abraham Joshua Heschel* (New York: Macmillan Publishing Co., 1985), wherein the author expresses his disagreement with Fackenheim and other critics who claim that Heschel does not advance philosophical argumentation for the religious views he espouses.
4. Cf. *Conservative Judaism* 23 (Fall 1968), 12–24.
5. Abraham J. Heschel, *Man Is Not Alone: A Philosophy of Religion* (New York: Farrar, Straus, and Young, 1951), pp. 77–78. Hereafter cited as *Not Alone*.
6. Edward K. Kaplan, "Mysticism and Despair in Abraham J. Heschel's Religious Thought," *The Journal of Religion* 57 (January 1977), p. 39.
7. *Not Alone*, p. 71.
8. Abraham J. Heschel, *God in Search of Man: A Philosophy of Judaism* (New York: Farrar, Straus, and Cudahy, 1955), p. 138.
9. Abraham J. Heschel, *The Prophets* (New York: Harper and Row, 1962), pp. 435–440.
10. *Not Alone*, pp. 259–260, 249–251.

7

Heschel's Poetics of Religious Thinking

EDWARD K. KAPLAN

Any interpreter of Heschel faces a double task: (1) to penetrate his thought and organize it into some conceptual order; that is, to systematize philosophical and theological insights dispersed amidst emotionally charged—and often baroque—poetic prose; and (2) to experience intuitively the power and depth of his expressive prose in order to possess, as it were, the writer's own spiritual experience. Heschel's theory and use of poetic language brings us to the heart of his endeavor. We must appreciate and respond personally, as well as understand. This philosopher is a man of prayer who seeks to open our minds to our hearts, to reconcile the rational and artistic dimensions of religious life, and thus to prepare us to meet God directly.

Heschel's expository style is essentially pragmatic. It is easy to be either stymied or inspired, more challenging to distinguish between his several modes of discourse and then, consciously and critically, to integrate them. But the method is clear: read with empathy and imaginative participation while not confusing his different means: rational argumentation; theological and philosophical aphorism;

esthetic evocation; and spiritual insight. Heschel's rhetorical approaches are complex and sophisticated. What has sometimes disparagingly been called "beautiful style" lends experiential substance to formulations that might otherwise strike only the surface of the mind.

Heschel's entire opus constitutes an apologetics which seeks not only to convince but moreso to transform our very consciousness of reality. In all his writings, rich imagery collaborates with incisive reasoning in order to wrench our minds, often quite violently, from commonly accepted categories to new patterns of religious thinking. I stress the dynamic term "religious thinking" as opposed to philosophical "thought."[1] Heschel does not claim that any rational method or theological system can adequately prove God's reality. Quite the contrary. His philosophical arguments consistently undermine the pride and prejudices of speculation in which rationality seeks to fit God into its preestablished concepts.

Heschel prepares us to think religiously by first overthrowing our usual self-centered manner of thinking in which we conceive of the self as a subject in search of its ultimate object, God. Described structurally, the basic principle of "religious thinking" is the *"recentering" of subjectivity from the person to God.* Heschel combines various modes of discourse so that, as did the prophets, we may penetrate "a divine understanding of a human situation. Prophecy, then, may be described as *exegesis of existence from a divine perspective.*"[2] We would read the Bible, for example, not to learn about Israel's search for the divine, but rather to gain insight into God's active pursuit of His errant people; the Bible is not human theology, but God's anthropology.[3] Ultimately we should fathom and judge ourselves as images of the divine, privileged objects of God's concern burdened with fearsome responsibilities.

God is the Subject

Heschel's journey toward faith is diametrically opposed to that of traditional philosophy. His model is the Hebrew Bible, not subsequent Greek elaborations: "It was not the aspiration of Israel to know the Absolute but to ascertain what He asks of man; to commune with His will rather than with His essence."[4] But what of modern seekers, to whom God no longer speaks directly? Heschel considers revelation to be continuous and assumes that the divine still manifests itself: "Man cannot see God, but man can be seen by God. He is not the object of a discovery but the subject of revelation."[5] In *Man Is Not Alone* (1951), Heschel traces the entire process of transformation. The decisive point occurs in chapter 9, "In the Presence of God" (pp. 67–79), which highlights the moment of transition from the mind emptied to a revelation on God's part to our consciousness. A remarkable passage evokes this ecstatic invasion of divine insight:

> Apathy turns to splendor unawares. The ineffable has shuddered itself into the soul. It has entered our consciousness like a ray of light passing into a lake. Refraction of that ray brings about a turning in our mind: we are penetrated by His insight. We cannot think any more as if He were there and we here. He is both there and here. He is not *a being,* but *being in and beyond all beings.*[6]

God is both transcendent and immanent, not a being out-there, beyond the world, but intimately present to all existence.

A life of worship is the best way to revise our relationship with God. Prayer can convert our consciousness of reality. That is why, in his luminous study, *Man's Quest for God* (1954), Heschel returns time and again to that recentering of subjectivity:

> We do not step out of the world when we pray; we merely see the world in a different setting. The self is not the hub, but the spoke of the revolving wheel. In prayer we shift the center of living from self-consciousness to self-surrender. God is the center toward which all forces tend.
>
> Prayer takes the mind out of the narrowness of self-interest, and enables us to see the world in a mirror of the holy. For when we betake ourselves to the extreme opposite of the ego, we can behold a situation from the aspect of God.[7]

Heschel describes a symmetrical shift from the self to God, one that he illustrates by the geometrical image of the wheel: God is the center and my self-awareness is a mere spoke. Such structural descriptions are handy, and their author takes them seriously, but these analogies strike only the surface of the mind.[8] This is why Heschel says that "poetry is to religion what analysis is to science, and it is certainly no accident that the Bible was not written *more geometrico* but in the language of poets."[9] Heuristic images teach us how to *think* about existence, but they do not help us integrate concepts and intuitions. Religious thinking transforms our emotions as well as our modes of perception.

The poetic elements of Heschel's style play an essential part in converting consciousness. His apologetic endeavor is founded upon a logical contradiction which he attempts to resolve through literary means. On the one hand, he conceptualizes theologically the divine-human relationship by using spatial analogies, the dynamic shift which is another Copernican recentering of our subjectivity. On the other hand, he strives to nurture the reader's religious insights by evoking his own experiences in beautiful passages that echo our loves, fears, and yearnings. Religious philosophy is the armature, poetry the flesh and blood.

The Spiritual Itinerary

Heschel organized his two central books—*Man Is Not Alone: A Philosophy of Religion* (1951) and *God in Search of Man: A Philosophy of Judaism* (1955)—according to the same strategy. Both ambitiously sweep through Western philosophy and Judaic tradition from the author's Kabbalistic-Hasidic perspective. The beginnings of both explore the sense of the ineffable and prepare our spiritual awareness of living as objects of God's concern. The author analyzes the experiences of awe, wonder, and radical amazement that should jar our thinking off the beaten track. The second half of each book reinterprets common moral and religious principles in the light of transformed consciousness. At all stages, the author uses poetic devices to insinuate theological intuitions into his demonstration.

The general structure of *Man Is Not Alone* typifies the itinerary. Part One, "The Problem of God," consists of 17 chapters (pp. 1–176) that depict and analyze phenomenologically the radical conversion to faith. Part Two, "The Problem of Living," consisting of nine longer chapters (pp. 179–296), defines religion and morality from an essentially Jewish perspective—one derived from inner experience as well as from written tradition.[10] I shall concentrate on Part One.[11] The first eight chapters prepare readers for the revelation (which might also be considered a mystical insight). The goal is reached in chapter 9 when Heschel evokes the discovery that we are objects of God's concern.

Heschel's theory of language organizes his thinking about the divine and its relationship to the mundane. Paradoxically, he builds his system upon what we cannot truly express. Chapter 1, "The Sense of the Ineffable," introduces the fundamental incongruity between words and subtle or exceptional experiences. The ineffable is an *a priori* category of his philosophy, "as if there were an *imperative*, a compulsion to pay attention to that which lies beyond our grasp" (p. 4).[12] As a corollary, the philosopher considers creative activity to be inspired, in large part, by awareness of our limits:

> What characterizes man is not only his ability to develop words and symbols, but also his being compelled to draw a distinction between the utterable and the unutterable, to be stunned by that which is but cannot be put into words. . . . The attempt to convey what we see and cannot say is the everlasting theme of mankind's unfinished symphony (p. 4).

The metaphor of "mankind's unfinished symphony" names a familiar artistic work in order to arouse our yearning for the transcendent.

This preliminary definition of the ineffable dimension of human experience, completed by the symphonic metaphor, directs our thought toward that which lies beyond. Heschel enlarges our ideas about what is real and questions all preconceptions: "Wonder, radical amazement, the state of maladjustment to words and notions, is a prerequisite for an authentic awareness of that which is" (p. 11). He wants to convince us that reality embraces more than what we normally know, and to foster our own radical amazement.

Heschel then endows the beyond with specific meaning and value. He makes another conceptual leap: "What we encounter in our perception of the sublime, in our radical amazement, is a spiritual suggestiveness of reality, an *allusiveness* to transcendent meaning. . . . We are struck with an awareness of the immense preciousness of being" (p. 22). The reverence provoked by the ineffable demonstrates that such meaning exists. The "logical" path he has followed thus far can be summarized: (1) the world is perceived as an allusion, (2) specifically, to transcendent meaning, (3) the content of which is the world's preciousness. The author's conclusion is axiomatic, "a *certainty without knowledge:* it is real without being expressible" (p. 22).

The crucial transition occurs in chapter 5, "Knowledge by Appreciation." Heschel's discourse becomes less intellectually incisive and more poetic; philosophy yields its authority to emotionally charged analogies. The poetry of his style makes us increasingly conscious of positive feelings of appreciation contained within our sense of the ineffable. Distinctions between ordinary thinking and religious insight become clearer:

> What is extraordinary appears to us as habit, the dawn a daily routine of nature. But time and again we awake. In the midst of walking in the never-ending procession of days and nights, we are suddenly filled with a solemn terror, with a feeling of our wisdom being inferior to dust. We cannot endure the heartbreaking splendor of sunsets. Of what avail, then, are opinions, words, dogmas? In the confinement of our study rooms, our knowledge seems to us a pillar of light. But when we stand at the door which opens out to the infinite, we realize that all concepts are but glittering motes that populate a sunbeam (p. 35).

This important passage illustrates how Heschel uses poetic devices to clinch his philosophical demonstrations. He personifies the normal passage of time as "the never-ending procession of days and nights." The analysis is already tinted with emotion. His expression of "wisdom as inferior to dust" uses a biblical image of mortality to concretize the finitude of human knowledge. The ideas climax *suddenly* with an outbreak of "solemn terror." The dictionary helps us to unpack the complexity of this insight realized through emotions: "terror" is a state of extreme fear, dread, devastating insecurity; whereas "solemn" softens the horror with a touch of awe; religious ceremonies are "solemn." The word "splendid" appears in definitions of "solemn" and, in fact, enters in the next sentence: "We cannot endure the heartbreaking splendor of sunsets." Of course this sentence does not mean exactly what it says; the author does not collapse. The purpose of this hyperbole, and the glorious image, is to evoke awe toward unfathomable creation. Sunrise and sunset no longer appear as monotonous cyclical processes but recall the miraculous death and rebirth of existence. The conceptual breakthrough is indeed terrifying because it confronts us with all-surpassing mystery.

The poetic dimension of this passage probes the subtle modalities of our inner life and awakens not-yet-conscious insights. This is the chapter of *Man Is Not Alone* in which Heschel insists that "poetry is to religion what analysis is to science" (p. 37, cited above). It is significant that a contrast between our knowledge as "a pillar of light" which becomes "glittering motes that populate a sunbeam" closes the paragraph neatly. These images, because of their picturesque loveliness, mitigate the shock of our mind's sudden humiliation.

This frightful abandonment of reassuring notions also strengthens our consent to the sacred. Radical amazement bridges the chasm between our minds and ultimate meaning. Admiration, reverence, and awe make us increasingly appreciate the mystery in which we participate. Now that he has begun to transform our self-centered categories, Heschel polemicizes the subject/object split in order finally to reject that manner of thinking:

> Our self-assured mind specializes in producing knives, as if it were a cutlery, and in all its thoughts it flings a blade, cutting the world in two: in a thing and in a self; in an object and in a subject that conceives the object as distinct from itself. A mercenary of our will to power, the mind is trained to assail in order to plunder rather than to commune in order to love (p. 38).

Heschel dramatizes the banal epistemological fact of a subject that requires an object of consciousness in order to think. Reason appears as a sadistic butcher and the process of concept formation as imperialistic attacks launched to gratify our will to power. The graphic imagery again injects value judgments into an otherwise logical argumentation. However, the polemic style should not divert us from the real lesson: Communion is a higher form of knowledge.

The person who thinks religiously overcomes the subject/object split. Humility reconciles us with the universe so that we can view the self, not as an antagonist but as a member of a cosmic fellowship:

> Where man meets the world, not with the tools he has made but with the soul with which he was born; not like a hunter who seeks his prey but like a lover to reciprocate love; where man and matter meet as equals before the mystery, both made, maintained and destined to pass away, it is not an object, a thing that is given to his sense, but a state of fellowship that embraces him and all things (p. 38).

The harmony of Heschel's flowing, rhythmical sentence reinforces the message. Thinking displaces its focus from *objects* to *a state of being* in which an individual feels at home in the universe. The turning of the mind firmly distinguishes the hunter pursuing his prey from the lover yearning to reciprocate affection freely proffered. Mankind and matter are "equals before the mystery," finite and mortal.

Religious thinking begins when the self leaves the center: "*To* our knowledge the world and the 'I' are two, an object and a subject; but *within* our wonder the world and the 'I' are one in being, in eternity. We become alive to our living in the great fellowship of all beings" (p. 39). Communion is a prerequisite of religious awareness; we sense our kinship with the visible cosmos and feel its spiritual unity. An unheard of significance begins to penetrate our consciousness: "Things surrounding us emerge from the triteness with which we have endowed them, and their strangeness opens like a void between them and our mind, a void that no words can fill" (p. 39). The "void" is more than the inevitable phenomenological gap between consciousness and its contents; it is an uncanny feeling for the true incommensurability between the mystery and our mind. The "strangeness" is our sense of estrangement from the Absolute.

Intuitions of estrangement lead us to analyze the structure of thought itself: "The self is more than we dream of; it stands, as it were, with its back to the mind. Indeed, to the mind even the mind itself is more enigmatic than a star" (p. 45). We have clarified the mind's function; now we question its meaning and origin. Heschel compares thought with a star in order to concretize his abstract analogy. The image of an "enigmatic" star appeals to poetic appreciation at least as much as to scientific curiosity.

Heschel makes another conceptual leap by introducing the divine foundation, a will of which our intelligence is but an echo. What is mystery to us alludes to superior truth. The self's enigma reflects the presence of a higher self, God, the source of human self-consciousness:

> Once we discover that the self *in itself* [italics added] is a monstrous deceit, that the self is something transcendent in disguise, we begin to feel the pressure that keeps us down to a mere self. We begin to realize that our normal consciousness is in a state of trance, that what is higher in us is usually suspended. We begin to feel like strangers within our normal consciousness, as if our own will were imposed upon us (p. 47).

Heschel places a theological insight in the chasm he has made us feel within consciousness. He magnifies the self's imponderability by polarizing two views: "the self *in itself* is a monstrous deceit" while a broader view perceives the self as "something transcendent in disguise."

At the end of chapter 6, "A Question Beyond Words," Heschel makes the final step from a mode of thinking centered on self to one centered from God:

Upon the level of normal consciousness I find myself wrapt in self-consciousness and claim that my acts and states originate in and belong to myself. But in penetrating and exposing the self, I realize that the self did not originate in myself, that the essence of the self is in its being a non-self, that ultimately man is not a subject but an *object**[13] (p. 48).

The breakthrough is complete.[14] Until chapter 5, Heschel the philosopher criticizes the finite self that asks questions about God; he does this in order to undermine our self-confidence, shatter our self-centered epistemology, and make plausible the idea of God as the origin of thought itself as well as of Being. We can now think about God and our world of experience from a biblical perspective.

A Poetics of Religious Language

Words, more than concepts, are the locus of our consciousness transformation. The most stimulating paradox of Heschel's endeavor is that he uses words to help us conceive, and ultimately to experience, the sacred reality beyond words.[15] That is why, in *God in Search of Man* and *The Prophets*, Heschel takes great pains to analyze the poetic function of biblical language. The prophets used figurative discourse as a tool, to convey verbally their essentially ineffable encounters with the living God. Their words mix the divine and the human, as does the event that produced them: "The spirit of God is set in the language of man, and who shall judge what is content and what is frame?"[16]

Statements about the sacred are necessarily metaphorical, simultaneously conveying similarity and otherness, a mixture of human and divine. In I. A. Richards' terminology, the metaphor is a concrete image which alludes to another reality, based on some analogy between the two. The metaphorical "vehicle" appears in the text, while the "tenor" remains absent or implicit. The tenor of biblical metaphor is its divine component and God its only "true" content. Heschel interprets the phrase "God spoke" in this light: *"What is literally true to us is a metaphor compared with what is metaphysically real to God."*[17] This is one way of asserting the transcendent reality of the tenor (i.e., God) while affirming the contingent nature of language. Statements about encounters with God are "understatements" of

sacred fact: "The speech of God is not less but more than literally
real."[18] Heschel characterizes religious assertions as understatements
to emphasize that which lies beyond words. His theory displaces the
usual focus from the negativity of language to its metaphysically
positive God-side.

For Heschel, poetic language bridges the esthetic and the religious.
In a passage that typifies his own practice, he firmly differentiates
between two distinct uses of language:

> *Descriptive* words stand in a fixed relation to conventional and
> definite meanings, such as the concrete nouns, chair, table, or the
> terms of science; and *indicative* words stand in a fluid relation to
> ineffable meanings and, instead of describing, merely intimate
> something we cannot fully comprehend. The content of such
> words as God, time, beauty, eternity cannot be faithfully imagined
> or reproduced in our minds. Still they convey a wealth of meaning
> to our sense of the ineffable. Their function is not to call up a
> definition in our minds but to introduce us to a reality which they
> signify.[19]

In *Man's Quest for God* he explores how indicative words, when
construed flexibly as metaphors, can empower our minds:

> A word is a focus, a point at which meanings meet and from which
> meanings seem to proceed. In prayer, as in poetry, we turn to the
> words, not to use them as signs for things, but to see things in the
> light of the words. . . . The word is stronger than the will.[20]

Poetically construed language displaces our awareness from the self to
the text. Words can then seize the initiative and transform the soul.

Poetry becomes powerful when it probes the experiential founda-
tions of our thinking. Heschel's expressive style appeals to our
passions and revives memories and desires with which they re-
verberate:

> Even when our thinking about it [the ultimate question] takes
> place on a discursive level our memory must remain moored to our
> perceptions of the ineffable, and our mind abide in a state of awe
> without which we never acquire a common language with the spirit
> of the question, without which the original nature of the problem
> will not disclose itself to us.
>
> The issue at stake will be apprehended only by those who are

able to find categories that mix with the unalloyed and to forge the imponderable into unique expression.[21]

Logically, it is impossible to "find categories that mix with the unalloyed," for the unalloyed is, by definition, unadulterated, pure— utterly transcendent. But poetically, the task is possible.

The religious writer combines the poetic with the propositional, harmonizes discursive reasoning with spiritual intuitions, so that our minds may "abide in a state of awe." Awe is a form of religious thinking that embraces both the human-side and the divine-side of religious perception—just as biblical metaphor contains within its unity of differences both frames of reference. At one and the same time, we intuit God's presence and His otherness: "It is the tension of the known and the unknown, of the common and the holy, of the nimble and the ineffable, that fills the moments of our insights."[22]

Two paragraphs from the section of chapter 9 of *Man Is Not Alone* entitled "The Dawn of Faith" illustrate how Heschel's indicative language fleshes out the skeleton of religious thinking and plumbs our emotional depths. Each paragraph consists of two parallel sentences, while the section as a whole works like a prose poem, arousing our sense of wonder within a clear conceptual framework. Prior to the paragraphs in question, the author explicitly points us "to a plane . . . where His presence may be defied but not denied, and where, at the end, faith in Him is the only way" (p. 68). The first paragraph depicts the intuition and interprets it in structural terms while the second one reinforces the message with imagery:

> Once our bare soul is exposed to the omnipresence of the ineffable, we cannot bid it cease to shatter us with its urging wonder. It is as if there were only signs and hidden reminders of the one and only true subject, of whom the world is a cryptic object.
>
> Who lit the wonder before our eyes and the wonder of our eyes? Who struck the lightning in the minds and scorched us with an imperative of being overawed by the holy as unquenchable as the sight of the stars? (p. 68).

Dramatic words in the first paragraph make abstractions concrete: Our "soul" is *bare, exposed* and appears to the mind's eye as a vulnerable naked body. The "ineffable" is *omnipresent* and *shatters* us; its "wonder" is *urging*, endowed with stubborn desire. The second sentence interprets these evocations of the ineffable, beginning with an analogy: "It is *as if there were* [italics added] only signs and hidden reminders . . . "; the explanation appears at the end: "the one and only true subject, of whom the world is a cryptic object." Emotions feed back into the concept of subject and object, while the term "cryptic object" suggests the world's spiritual dimension.

The second paragraph translates the code. Heschel prepares the answer by asking specific questions: "Who lit the wonder before our eyes and the wonder of our eyes?" One single sentence juxtaposes the world's wonder and the marvel of my very consciousness of the world: "*before* our eyes and *of* our eyes." The world and my eyes witness the same mystery. Both sentences—"Who lit the wonder . . ." and "Who struck the lightning . . . ?"—thrust us into the beyond. Dramatic verbs make this intuition of the divine presence feel concrete: God "*struck* the lightning . . . and *scorched* us with an imperative." The abstract philosophical term "imperative" vibrates throughout our bodies while the repeated s sounds reinforce the impact. Our innate sense of God's reality should burst forth as would a bolt of lightning, a traditional image of intellectual or mystical illumination.[23] The picture again relates Heschel's extraordinarily keen wonderment to a secular reader's experience and helps us to become "overawed by the holy as unquenchable as the sight of the stars." In the realm of logical prose, thirst is unquenchable, not star-gazing. This endless thirst, however, is spiritual, not gastric. To the poet—as to many of us—stars are heavenly bodies, and cosmic infinity a mystery to be revered.

Heschel's rich style recreates the complexity of religious consciousness. His condensed juxtaposition, and even mixture, of thinking and feeling lifts to our awareness moral and spiritual yearnings which might otherwise remain tacit, unconscious and uninterpreted. The author's sensitivity certainly derives from his encounters with the sacred while we, thirsting, aspire toward his faith. His eloquence should nurture the "hunger of the heart" which many consider to be evidence of God's presence within us.[24] Heschel's metaphors and analogies respond to and excite our unconscious loves and lacks, while, at the same time, they point beyond the merely human to the God-side of the expressed encounter. This co-presence of opposite ontological contexts is faith's dynamic tension: "For to have faith is to abide rationally outside, while spiritually within, the mystery" (p. 54).

The Endless Tension

The "poetic beauty" of Heschel's style derives from this internal contradiction between the finite world evoked by language and the transcendent Reality to which it alludes. Our minds remain both inside and outside the mystery which sanctifies the world. Our quest for the Absolute—be it a personal God, Presence, or Being—endows our reading with an elusive but compelling urgency. Most significantly, the writer's verbal grace ushers us *beyond the beautiful into a sacred realm:*

> Wonder is not a state of esthetic enjoyment. Endless wonder is endless tension, a situation in which we are shocked at the inadequacy of our awe, at the weakness of our shock, as well as the state of being asked the ultimate question (pp. 68–69).

Religious thinking maintains the "endless tension" between spiritual hunger and esthetic gratification.

Heschel's apologetic goal—as I suggested at the outset—is to make us undergo the disparity between our minds and the sacred so that we surrender to God's initiative. The decisive turning point of *God in Search of Man* (chapter 13) evokes and interprets even more explicitly than chapter 9 of *Man Is Not Alone* the moment of despair in which the mind completely relinquishes common thought, to the extreme point of losing language itself:

> Only those who have gone through days on which words were of no avail, on which the most brilliant theories jarred the ear like mere slang; only those who have experienced ultimate not-knowing, the voicelessness of a soul struck with wonder, total muteness, are able to enter the meaning of God, a meaning greater than the mind.[25]

This is probably the most terrifying challenge of Heschel's spiritual itinerary: to risk one's very reason in the pursuit of absolute truth. The rhythmic harmony of this representation of "ultimate not-knowing" forces sensitive readers to probe their horrifying distance from ultimate meaning. We are frail, miserable, and yet, as Heschel also asserts, inspired with "voiceless wonder."

Heschel's impressive certainty thus emerges from despair. We must first become utterly helpless, silence our ego-centered thinking before God can speak to us through religious texts:

> We must first peer through the darkness, feel strangled and entombed in the hopelessness of living without God, before we are ready to feel the presence of His living light.
>
> "And it shall come to pass, when I bring a cloud over the earth,

that the bow shall be seen in the cloud" (Genesis 9:14). When ignorance and confusion blot out all thoughts, the light of God may suddenly burst forth in the mind like a rainbow in the sky. Our understanding of the greatness of God comes about as an act of illumination.[26]

This extraordinary passage exemplifies the way in which Heschel's poetic style churns up almost unbearable feelings which he then translates into a theological insight. The Bible's authority can then give the seeker confidence. The quotation places individual anxiety within tradition, so that anguish melts away in the arms of a community.

The chapters of *Man Is Not Alone* and *God in Search of Man* which evoke revelation are followed by chapters that stress an equally crucial corrective: exceptional moments of insight must become part of a fabric of biblical theology. The final chapter of Part One of *God in Search of Man*—entitled "Beyond Insight" (chapter 16)—underlines the necessity of interpretation: "Private insights and inspirations prepare us to accept what the prophets convey. They enable us to understand the question to which revelation is the answer." The final chapter of Part One of *Man Is Not Alone*—similarly entitled "Beyond Faith" (chapter 17)—definitively formulates the relationship between intuition and systematic thinking:

> The insights of faith are general, vague and stand in need of conceptualization in order to be communicated to the mind, integrated and brought to consistency. Reason is a necessary coefficient of faith, lending form to what often becomes violent, blind and exaggerated by imagination. *Faith without reason is mute; reason without faith is deaf.*[28]

Heschel's eloquence, when read with the sympathetic discernment of religious thinking, becomes alive with God's presence. Concretely we sense what it might be like to experience the world with divine concern. Even someone bereft of faith can glimpse in his celebration of human holiness a homeland worth the strife. At the very least, by his analysis of language and his masterful exercise of its literary potentials, Heschel nurtures our attachment to the ultimate. Words can open the door or may themselves remain locked:

> Our problem, then, is how to share the certainty of Israel that the Bible contains that which God wants us to know and to hearken

to; how to attain a collective sense for the presence of God in the biblical words. In this problem lies the dilemma of our fate, and in the answer lies the dawn or the doom.[29]

Notes

1. Cf. Emil Fackenheim's astute criticisms of *Man Is Not Alone* in *Judaism* 1 (January 1952), 85–89, and of *God In Search of Man* in *Conservative Judaism* 20 (Fall 1966), 50–53, in which he distinguishes between Heschel's stated philosophical task to erect a system and Heschel as a phenomenologist of "religious thinking" more interested in its dynamics. Fackenheim is mistaken to separate the different modes of Heschel's discourse and to reject the conceptual in favor of the expressive. Cf. Edward K. Kaplan, "Form and Content in A. J. Heschel's Poetic Style," *Central Conference of American Rabbis Journal* 28 (April 1971), 28–39; Avraham Holtz, "Religion and the Arts in the Theology of A. J. Heschel," *Conservative Judaism* 28 (Fall 1973), 27–39; David Hartman, *The Breakdown of Tradition and the Quest for Renewal* (Montreal: The Gate Press, 1980), pp. 40–54 on Heschel. For some important theoretical background see Frank B. Brown, "Transfiguration: Poetic Metaphor and Theological Reflection," *The Journal of Religion* 62 (January 1982), 29–56, which develops a theory that integrates propositional theology and metaphor and provides a useful bibliography.
2. Abraham Joshua Heschel, *The Prophets* (New York: Harper and Row, 1962), p. xiv. I have explored the consequences of this notion (which I had called the *displacement* of subjectivity) in two articles: "Language and Reality in Abraham J. Heschel's Philosophy of Religion," *Journal of the American Academy of Religion* 41 (March 1973), 94–113; and "Mysticism and Despair in Abraham J. Heschel's Religious Thought," *The Journal of Religion* 57 (January 1977), 33–47; cf. also, Maurice Friedman, "Divine Need and Human Wonder: The Philosophy of Abraham J. Heschel," *Judaism* 25 (Winter 1976), 65–68, esp. pp. 72–74.
3. Cf. Abraham Joshua Heschel, *Man Is Not Alone* (New York: Farrar, Straus and Young, 1951), p. 129; hereafter cited as *Not Alone*.
4. *Ibid.*
5. *Ibid.*
6. *Ibid.*, p. 78. For a detailed analysis of this passage see my article, "Mysticism and Despair," *op. cit.*, pp. 38–42. Heschel evokes a similar moment of illumination in *God in Search of Man* (New York: Farrar, Straus and Cudahy, 1955), hereafter cited as *Search*, chapter 13 (esp. pp. 140–141), which holds a similarly decisive place in the book's apologetic structure; see below.
7. Abraham Joshua Heschel, *Man's Quest for God: Studies in Prayer and Symbolism* (New York: Charles Scribner's Sons, 1954), p. 7; hereafter cited in the text as *Quest*. From among numerous references to the

"recentering" of subjectivity, the following from *Not Alone* are especially interesting: pp. 48, 64, 109, 120, 126, 215, 281–282.

8. Cf. *Not Alone*, p. 225: "Life is tridimensional, every act can be evaluated by two coordinate axes, the abscissa is man, the ordinate God. Whatever man does to man, he also does to God." Cf. *Ibid.*, pp. 47, 137.

9. *Ibid.*, p. 37.

10. Three crucial chapters of *Not Alone* were published much earlier in periodicals: the final chapter, "The Pious Man," in the *Review of Religion* 6 (1942), 293–307, entitled "An Analysis of Piety"; parts of chapter 17, "Beyond Faith" (pp. 159–171), the final chapter of Part One and chapter 22, "What is Religion?" (pp. 229–240), in *The Journal of Religion* 23 (April 1943), 117–124, as "The Holy Dimension," and in *The Reconstructionist* 10 (Nov. 13, 1944), 10–14, and *Ibid.*, 10 (Nov. 17, 1944), 12–16, as "Faith." Heschel clearly knew where he was going.

11. Hereafter, the page number(s) placed in parentheses at the end of a quotation will refer to *Not Alone*.

12. From a philosophical perspective, Heschel's *a priori* reasoning weakens his demonstration: cf. p. 19: "a universal insight into an objective aspect of reality, of which all men are at all times capable." Cf. also pp. 62, 84, 89, 98, 104, 199, 222, 247, for other explicitly stated *a prioris*.

13. Heschel's footnote (indicated by the asterisk) refers to p. 128, part of chapter 14, "God Is the Subject" (pp. 125–133).

14. At this decisive point in the book, Heschel interrupts the itinerary and steps backward. In chapter 7 he attempts to refute "The God of the Philosophers." In the following chapter, he returns to the notion of God's subjectivity (chapter 8, "The Ultimate Question").

15. But is that not the source of all culture? "Music, poetry, religion—they all originate in the soul's encounter with an aspect of reality for which reason has no concepts and language no means" (*Not Alone*, p. 36). This important sentence seems to contain a misprint, the only one I have found in Heschel's works; I have replaced the word "initiate" with "originate." One might also read: "they all initiate the soul's encounter with. . . ."

16. *Search*, p. 259. For a more detailed discussion of the following see my article, "Language and Reality in A. J. Heschel's Philosophy of Religion," esp. pp. 103–106.

17. *Search*, p. 180.

18. *Ibid.*

19. *Ibid.*, pp. 180–181. Cf. the entire chapter 17, "The Prophetic Under-statement," pp. 176–183.

20. *Quest*, p. 26; cf. p. 47.

21. *Not Alone*, p. 60. The role of memory in liturgical prayer should be studied in depth. For a start see *Quest*, p. 30; "The power which streams from words unites itself with the elemental power that rises from memory. Thoughts are being transcended, experiences of the past illumined, desires transformed. A thought becomes a wish, a desire a demand, a demand an expectation, an expectation a vision. These steps represent at once stages of personal attitude as well as objective events."

22. *Not Alone*, p. 61.
23. Cf. *Ibid.*, p. 78: "But, then, a moment comes like a thunderbolt, in which a flash of the undisclosed rends our dark apathy asunder."
24. Cf. Howard Thurman, *Disciplines of the Spirit* (New York: Harper and Row, 1963): "'The givenness of God' in the hunger of the heart. This is native to personality, and when it becomes part of a man's conscious focus it is prayer at its best and highest. It is the movement of the heart toward God; a movement that in some sense is with God" (p. 87). Cf. *Not Alone*: "Some men go on a hunger strike in the prison of the mind, starving for God. There is a joy, ancient and sudden, in this starving. There is a reward, a grasp of the intangible, in the flaming reverie breaking through bars of thought" (p. 90); also: "God's existence can never be tested by human thought. All proofs are mere demonstrations of our thirst for Him. Does the thirsty one need proof of his thirst?" (p. 94).
25. *Search*, p. 140.
26. *Ibid.*
27. *Ibid.*, p. 164.
28. *Not Alone*, p. 173. This renews a famous Kantian dictum: "Thoughts without content are empty, intuitions without concepts are blind" (*Critique of Pure Reason*, A51, B75, p. 93 of Kemp-Smith edition). My thanks to Professor David Wong for this reference.
29. *Search*, p. 246; cf. *Ibid.*, pp. 252–253.

PART
FOUR

Heschel as Social Critic and Ecumenist

8

"Some Are Guilty, All Are Responsible"
Heschel's Social Ethics

ROBERT MCAFEE BROWN

A Confession: Personal Positioning

In the words of that great Jewish theologian, Groucho Marx, "Before I begin my speech, there is something important I want to say." The location of this symposium in Benedictine country in central Minnesota is extremely important to me, and shapes the character of much that I want to say. Thirty years ago, while teaching at Macalester College in St. Paul, I had occasion to work for the re-election of a young Congressman named Eugene McCarthy. Up to that time in my life, my only exposure to Roman Catholicism had been—I say it merely descriptively—the Cardinal Spellman variety regnant in the archdiocese of New York City where I lived. After the election, Gene and Abigail McCarthy took my wife and me to visit St. John's Abbey, where Gene had once been a novice, and meeting Fr. Godfrey Diekmann and others like him became the occasion of my ecumenical conversion. The depth of that conversion can be measured by the fact that a few months later I returned for another visit, and spent my ninth wedding anniversary alone in a Benedictine cell—a fact that scored me a few points on the ecumenical frontier but no noticeable points at home.

That was the beginning of a pilgrimage that later took me to Rome as a Protestant observer at Vatican II. One of my most important encounters in Rome was with Heschel himself, who had come over in great agitation at the rough weather the conciliar statement on the Jews was encountering. I spent a long evening with him in his hotel room, after which I submitted an equally long intervention of my own concerns to the Secretariat for Christian Unity. Monsignor (now Cardinal) Willebrands, after reading my comments, asked, not in hostility but out of interest, "Tell me, have you by any chance been talking with Rabbi Heschel"? There was a man who knew how to get back to the sources.

In a much deeper sense, my experiences in Collegeville and Rome helped me to "get back to the sources." For I soon discovered that to take the Protestant-Catholic dialogue seriously meant taking the Jewish-Christian dialogue equally seriously. For how could we Protestants and Catholics understand one another if we did not understand our common heritage in Judaism? It was not enough to go back to the Reformation, or the early so-called "undivided church," or even to the New Testament. We had to go back to our common source in the Hebrew Scriptures, and then re-discover, coincidentally, that Judaism had not disappeared shortly after the writing of the book of Malachi, but was alive and vigorous in the present as well, despite being the victim of a lot of heavy-handed Christian oppression in the intervening 2,000 years. Heschel became the presence before whom I was always forced to remember that all branches of Christians have a common source more venerable than any one of them.

And all of it started for me in the St. Benedict's-St. Joseph/St. John's-Collegeville ambiance. So I am particularly happy to be *here* as a Protestant, under Benedictine auspices, to pay tribute to a Jew.[1]

A Conundrum: Mysticism and Ethics

Heschel's social ethics. . . . To me, the fact that encapsulates it all is the astonishing title Heschel had as a faculty member at Jewish Theological Seminary. He was Professor of Jewish Ethics and

Mysticism. Now we have a difficult enough time defining "ethics" by itself, and probably an even more difficult time defining "mysticism" by itself, let alone defining "Jewish." (And some of us have been teaching long enough so that we aren't even sure anymore how to define "professor.") But those are the easy problems. How are we to understand "mysticism *and* ethics"? Juxtaposed, rather than separated? A single curricular discipline rather than two separate curricular disciplines? A strange notion indeed, and really not something definable in abstract terms. Something, surely, definable only in terms of a some*one*, so that if we can't really define or describe how those disciplines are combined, we *can* point to someone whose life so combined them that either without the other would seem truncated, dismembered from a living organism that is insufficient without both. And that someone is Abraham Joshua Heschel.

A Clue: "Divine Pathos"

Our basic task, then, in dealing with Heschel's social ethics, is to assure that his outward, visible, passionate and active life of concern about poverty, racism, war, and oppression—his ethics—is adequately related to the inner roots of his devotion to God, Torah, faith, prayer, and the life of radical amazement—his mysticism. We cannot truly speak of either without speaking of both. And yet for systematic purposes, a division must be made. I think I have found a way to indicate the connection that will then leave us free to concentrate on the social ethics side without appearing to slight the personal, mystical side.

In *The Prophets*, that marvelous early work of Heschel's, to which we shall frequently refer, he deals, among other things, with the theme of "divine pathos"—a theme that Dr. Merkle has discussed in a preceding chapter. Heschel defines "divine pathos" in one place as "combining absolute selflessness with supreme concern for the poor and exploited."[2] He points out that this "can hardly be regarded as the attribution to God of human characteristics." For there is no human being, not even in the Bible, who could be characterized as "merciful, gracious, slow to anger, abundant in love and truth, keeping love to the thousandth generation." For Heschel, then, the idea of divine pathos "is a genuine insight into God's relatedness to man, rather than a projection of human traits into divinity."[3]

So to the degree that these are ever characteristics of human nature, Heschel insists, to just that degree we humans are endowed with attributes of the divine. His conclusion, characteristically reversing our usual ways of thinking, and calling for a whole new approach on our part, is the following: "God's unconditional concern for justice is not an anthropomorphism. Rather, man's concern for justice is a theomorphism."[4] To paraphrase, limply: Concern for justice is not a trait we project out of our own experience onto God; rather, concern for justice is a divine trait with which God endows us, so that to the degree that we embody justice, God takes form within us.

That, it seems to me, gives us a sufficient clue into Heschel's character, and into the astonishing unity in his own life, of the outward and the inward, the contemplative and the active, the pray-er and the doer, the mystic and the ethicist. Indeed, the whole thrust of his life and thought suggests that such distinctions are no longer truly possible. Their very employment is a transgression of what I offer as a new commandment: "Thou shalt not bifurcate the unbifurcatable."

John Bennett, commenting on this same passage from *The Prophets*, has said with great insight:

> I ask you who knew and loved Abraham Heschel: Does not that conviction bring unity to his life, between his deeply personal religious quest, his commitment as a man of faith and of disciplined religious observance, his theological reflection—and his public life so filled with action, with innumerable speeches, demonstrations, pleas to the consciences of his fellow citizens, to public officials for the sake of racial justice and for peace in Vietnam? His concern was a reflection of God's concern.[5]

It is this approach that made it possible for Heschel to respond to the world in an attitude of what he called "radical amazement," which is a synonym for wonder. It does not mean turning away from everyday experience (a temptation of some brands of mysticism), but rather *being open in a new way to every aspect of experience*. There are three ways, he writes, in which we may respond to the reality of the world around us: "We may exploit it, we may enjoy it, we may accept it with awe."[6] Our generation has reached new heights (or depths) in its ability to *exploit*, and Heschel could have told us long ago about what we are now seeing to be the results of an attitude that makes the rape of the earth possible as the privilege of those with power.

It is surely an advance to suggest that rather than exploiting nature we *enjoy* it, since those who seek to enjoy usually take care not to exploit and destroy the objects of their enjoyment. But Heschel pushes us to go further than that. Unless we not only enjoy, but also *accept it with awe*, we continue to treat nature in ways that ultimately debase not only the created order but the creatures who dwell within it. And it is the quality of awe—which includes wonder or radical amazement— that pervades Heschel's thought and life. If for Plato, philosophy begins in wonder, for Heschel, wonder is not something we find only at the beginning of the human quest and can dispense with as we fill in the gaps of our knowledge with more data. No, Heschel responds:

> To the prophets wonder is a *form of thinking*. It is not the beginning of knowledge but an act that goes beyond knowledge; it does not come to an end when knowledge is acquired; it is an attitude that never ceases. There is no answer in the world to man's radical amazement.[7]

A Model: Maimonides, and Some Consequences

Heschel's attention to social concerns can be pointed to in other ways as well. One of these is established in his early work on Maimonides, the great twelfth-century Jewish philosopher. As Byron Sherwin has reported, "In writing Maimonides' biography, Heschel anticipated his own autobiography."[8] For what Heschel discovered in Maimonides' life—a fact not so apparent to other students of the medieval thinker—was that Maimonides' interests moved in new directions in the last decade of his life: "from scholarship to social action, from metaphysics to ethics, from thoughts to deeds."[9] As Heschel himself put it in an essay on "The Last Days of Maimonides," after citing a long letter in which Maimonides discourages the visit of an erudite admirer by telling him that he now fills his days with practical activity:

> This is Maimonides' last metamorphosis: from metaphysics to medicine, from contemplation to practice, from speculation to the imitation of God. God is not only the object of knowledge; He is the example one is to follow. . . . Preoccupation with the concrete man and the effort to aid him in his suffering is now the form of religious devotion. . . . Contemplation of God and service to man are combined and become one.[10]

As he reflects more on the shift between Maimonides' earlier and later commitments, Heschel concludes:

In contrast to his earlier view that man's ultimate perfection is purely intellectual—it does not include either actions or moral qualities, but only knowledge—he now defines man's ultimate end as *the imitation of God's ways* and actions, namely, kindness, justice, righteousness.[11]

How audacious (as Heschel might put it)! God is to be our model. We are to imitate God. There is not only an analogy of *being* between ourselves and God, but an analogy of *doing*. "Man is called upon to act in the likeness of God. 'As He is merciful, be thou merciful.'"[12]

That we are called upon to imitate God, that the source of our social ethics does not derive from our understanding of who we are but from what God asks of us, that the Bible is not man's theology but God's anthropology[13]—all makes clear that for Heschel, put mildly, we are called into a partnership with God. Put radically, God needs us. The mild form is unexceptionable to Jew and Christian alike. But the radical form suggests a parting of the ways between Heschel and traditional Christianity, and thus is a place where traditional Christians need to listen to Heschel. Traditional Christianity has certainly emphasized the self-sufficiency of God. All things are ultimately dependent upon God, but God is not dependent on any thing. Many of us were brought up on the famous equation in William Temple's Gifford lectures:

The world − God = 0; God − the world = God.

Thus, we were taught, *our* lack of being would in no way impair the *divine* being.

Not so, Heschel says. God minus the world is a God diminished. God needs us; the fulfillment of the divine intention for the world cannot be accomplished apart from the work of God's children. Whether this be called a Pelagian or semi-Pelagian heresy (and I can think of nothing that would matter less to Heschel), God has placed us here in the midst of an unfinished creation, and has given us the task of helping to bring it to fulfillment. That is why we were created. That is the purpose of our lives. That is the content of our prayer. That is why our deeds and our prayers can never be separated. That is why intention and deed are both necessary. That is why there must be both *kavanah*, the right intention, and *mitsvah*, the actual deed. And here again we see how the outer and the inner come together for Heschel. For just as the contemplation about God leads to the doing of deeds, so the doing of deeds is one of the "starting points of contemplation about God."[14]

A Source: Hasidism

The stress on deeds is also Hasidic, and while there is not space to develop the roots of Heschel's social ethics in Hasidism, we must at least note that the Hasidic concern with the everyday, the exaltation of the here and now, the refusal to let people retreat into other-worldliness or mere book learning in this world, the acknowledgement that "dancing counts for more than prayers"—all this was so much in the marrow of Heschel's bones that it is almost impossible to separate who he was from the heritage he embodied.

The claim that we not only need God but that God needs us is likewise nurtured from Hasidic roots. As Heschel says in his book about Hasidism, *The Earth Is the Lord's:*

> The meaning of man's life lies in his perfecting the universe. He has to distinguish, gather, and redeem the sparks of holiness scattered throughout the darkness of the world. This service is the motive of all precepts and good deeds. Man holds the key that can unlock the chains fettering the Redeemer.[15]

Quintessentially Hasidic. Quintessentially Heschel.

In another context, when talking about "Religion and Race," Heschel says:

> The universe is done. The great masterpiece, still undone, still in the process of being created, is history. For accomplishing his grand design, God needs the help of man. Man is and has the instrument of God, which he may or may not use in consonance with the grand design.[16]

With this view, Heschel contrasts theologies and philosophies of despair that tell us we can do nothing to change the course of history and must accept whatever providence metes out to us: "It was good that Moses did not study theology under the teachers of that message," he comments wryly, "otherwise, I would still be in Egypt building pyramids."[17]

Another characteristic of Hasidism is its humor, the device by which we are relieved of pretentions about ourselves, as though we had devised a good enough theology, or a good enough society, so that we could afford to relax. I want to share two instances of Heschel's humor, not only because they are a part of who he was, but also because they also illustrate this side of Hasidism. Both of them can be found in Byron Sherwin's book on Heschel. Sherwin cites a speech Heschel delivered at the annual convention of the American Medical Association—not a crowd particularly prone to responding to the prophetic voice. Heschel said, "The patient is haunted with fear, but some doctors are in a hurry, and above all, impatient. They have something in common with God; they cannot be easily reached, not even at the golf course."[18] And on the occasion of his inauguration as Visiting Professor at Union Theological Seminary, Heschel commented on those captivated by the then briefly-popular "death of God" movement, that they were like patients who found themselves very ill and began to scream, "The doctor is dead, the doctor is dead."[19]

A Vehicle: Scripture

Those who have known contemporary Hasidic Jews like Heschel or Elie Wiesel realize that there is no question, and no occasion, which cannot be illumined by the introductory phrase, "Let me tell you a story. . . ." Many of the stories come out of Hasidic lore or the Talmud. But there is usually a Scriptural base somewhere not too far below the surface, and one of the resources most used by Heschel was the Hebrew Bible. It was for him a source, like Hasidism, but equally a vehicle for sharing with others what he had found at the source. Steeped in the Bible from his early years, Heschel found it always speaking anew to contemporary situations. We cannot begin to understand his social ethics apart from this emphasis. His use of Scripture as a vehicle for insight into matters of social ethics was pervasive, and I will share an example from each of his two major lectures on religion and racism.

Heschel opened his talk at the National Conference on Religion and Race in Chicago in 1963 without equivocation:

At the first conference on religion and race, the main participants were Pharaoh and Moses. Moses' words were: "Thus says the Lord, the God of Israel, let My people go that they may celebrate a feast to Me." While Pharaoh retorted: "Who is the Lord, that I should heed this voice and let Israel go? I do not know the Lord, and moreover I will not let Israel go."

The outcome of that summit meeting has not come to an end. Pharaoh is not ready to capitulate. The exodus began, but is far from having been completed. In fact, it was easier for the children of Israel to cross the Red Sea than for a Negro to cross certain university campuses.[20]

Here the connection is direct, immediate, relentless. We are not allowed to dwell in the past, contemplating racial injustice in another era. The look at the past plunges us into the present, contemplating racial injustice today.

The same thing happened a year later when Heschel addressed the Metropolitan Conference on Religion and Race in New York City. Once more a biblical episode was used as the vehicle for an immediate and contemporary thrust. He takes us along with the children of Israel as they cross the Red Sea, and we share the sublime joy, the spiritual exaltation of that event. Not even Ezekiel, Heschel informs us, experienced such a sense of divine glory. And then, 3 days later, we are still with them, and they find no water. So they murmur against Moses, "What shall we drink"? Heschel:

> The episode seems shocking. What a comedown! Only three days earlier they had reached the highest peak of prophetic and spiritual exaltation, and now they complain about such a prosaic and unspiritual item as water. . . .

And then, without a pause, the transition is made from the distant past to the immediate present:

> The Negroes of America behave just like the children of Israel. Only in 1963, [i.e., a year ago] they experienced the miracle of having turned the tide of history, the joy of finding millions of Americans involved in the struggle for civil rights, the exaltation of fellowship, the March to Washington. Now only a few months later they have the audacity to murmur: "What shall we drink? We want adequate education, decent housing, proper employment." How ordinary, how unpoetic, how annoying![21]

Heschel goes on to describe the pleasant mood of the time:

> The Beatles have just paid us a visit. The AT&T is about to split its stock. Dividends are higher than ever. Castro is quiet and well-mannered. Russia is purchasing grain from us. Only the Negroes continue to disturb us: What shall we drink?[22]

Then he contrasts the occasional liberal identification and the demands of the long haul, in words that indict us all:

We are ready to applaud dramatic struggles once a year in Washington. For the sake of lofty principles we will spend a day or two in jail somewhere in Alabama.

But that prosaic demand for housing without vermin, for adequate schools, for adequate employment—right here in the vicinity of Park Avenue in New York City—sounds so trite, so drab, so banal, so devoid of magnificence.[23]

A Concentration: The Prophets

So we see how Heschel weaves individual Scripture passages into the fabric of his whole social message. But there is more to it than that, and the more is crucial. For it is this concern with trite things, minutiae, trivialities, that characterizes the whole of Scripture. Heschel has no use for Greek gods, contemplating eternal perfection in another realm. The God of the Bible, Heschel insists, "is described as reflecting over the plight of man rather than as contemplating eternal ideas."[24] And that theme, of course, comes particularly from the prophets:

> The prophet's field of concern is not the mysteries of heaven, the glories of eternity, but the blights of society, the affairs of the market place. . . . The predominant feature of the biblical pattern is unassuming, unheroic, inconspicuous piety, the sanctification of trifles, attentiveness to details.[25]

In *Israel: An Echo of Eternity*, Heschel develops the prophetic theme in another way: "The Hebrew Bible is not a book about heaven—it is a book about the earth. The Hebrew word *erets*, meaning earth, land, occurs at least five times as often in the Bible as the word *shamayim*, meaning heaven."[26]

Today we frequently hear Roman Catholic liberation theologians of Latin America accent a prophetic theme in their talk about "a preferential option for the poor," and God's own partiality for the oppressed. Listen to Heschel, at least 5 years before liberation theology had assumed even inchoate form: "The Bible insists that the interests of the poor have precedence over the interests of the rich. The prophets have a bias in favor of the poor."[27]

Only a few days before his death, responding to a question by a TV interviewer, Heschel pointed out a parallel between his own journey and that of Maimonides, who, as we recall, moved in his later years from speculation to action:

> I've written a book on the prophets on which I spent many years. And, really, this book changed my life. Because early in my life, my great love was for learning, studying. And the place where I preferred to live was my study and books and writing and thinking. I've learned from the prophets that I have to be involved in the affairs of man, in the affairs of suffering man.[28]

The difference between Heschel and Maimonides, was that Maimonides came to this point only in the last decade of his life, whereas it characterized Heschel for most of the decades of his life.

A Stance: Moral Madness

Let us highlight just one theme from the massive work on *The Prophets* that further explains Heschel's social passion. This is what he describes as the "moral madness" of the prophets. It is quite clear that in the eyes of their contemporaries, the prophets were looked upon as mad, and Heschel cites such Biblical characterizations in the cases of Hosea, Elisha, and Jeremiah, all of whom were considered madmen, who should, as is specifically recommended in the case of Jeremiah, be put "in the stocks and collar."[29]

Why do we call people "mad"? Because they see things from a perspective different than our own, which means that if they are right, we are wrong. Since we do not easily entertain the notion that we are wrong, we denominate our opponents as crazy, mad fools, if there is no other way left to dispose of them. And the prophets *do* do some very strange things: they call kings to account for injustice, they excoriate religious leaders for being co-opted, they announce the fulfillment of God's will through pagan leaders, they even rail against the God in whose name they presume to speak.

They are not psychotics, however. Heschel points up an important difference between prophet and psychotic. The psychotic crosses the threshhold into another world and finds it difficult, if not impossible, to return; whereas the prophet, confronted by a vision drawn from elsewhere, feels compelled to share the vision. As Heschel puts it: "The ideas he brings back to reality become a source of illumination of supreme significance to all other human beings."[30]

We dispose of such people, I have suggested, by calling them mad. But they leave us disturbed. And even though we, who share the majority viewpoint, upheld by the *status quo*, can confidently thrust aside these rude and uninviting fellows, and can tell ourselves that madness and sanity are determined by majority concensus, there still remains the nagging and disturbing question: *What if we have things reversed?* What if the minority viewpoint is, in fact, the true one? What if the ones we call mad are really sane? What if the rest of us are the ones who fail to see the world as it truly is?[31]

It was the burden and the glory of Heschel's life, I suggest, that he too had to wear this mantle of the prophet. He too had to proclaim the minority viewpoint. As he attempted to look at the world from a prophetic stance—in that daring notion of his that the prophet does not interpret God to the world but looks at the world through God's eyes—he was forced to take positions that many of his contemporaries thought demented and wrong and "mad." On no issue, perhaps, was this truer than on Vietnam. And his minority status was nowhere more evident than within the Jewish community itself, which did not appreciate Heschel's challenging the calculations of the Johnson administration, an administration that on more than one occasion sent emissaries to others in the Jewish community to say, none too gently, that unless Heschel cooled it, the Johnson administration might just diminish its military support to the State of Israel.

I do not think any of us in the Christian anti-war community knew that the price "Father Abraham" was paying for his alliance with us included not only his isolation from the mainstream of American thinking, but even more his isolation within the Jewish community. Fortunately, Heschel was more concerned to be faithful to the prophetic tradition than to court contemporary approval.

Nonconformity is the only place the prophet can feel at home. In this, Heschel was like his biblical namesake, for it was the task of the earlier Abraham not to conform, not to stay in the land where he "had it made," but in response to a divine mandate, to take off and go elsewhere in ways that must have made his contemporaries think him an utter fool. The biblical Abraham destroyed the idols of his father. And that has always been the prophetic task—the destruction of idols, the idols of nation, race, state, status, religion, whatever. Citing the experience of that earlier Abraham, the present-day Abraham said in one of his most powerful speeches, "Idols in the Temples" (in the temples, yet!): "Religion begins as a breaking off, as a going away. It continues in acts of nonconformity to idolatry."[32] Those words, written on a printed page, were also written with every human breath Heschel breathed.

A Consequence: Moral Outrage

I have chosen to emphasize moral madness as the stance most characteristic of the prophetic witness. But we must also note one of the consequences of that stance: moral outrage. How often Heschel's writings and speeches explode with the indignation so characteristic of his prophetic forebears. Here he is in the midst of the 1972 presidential campaign:

> If the prophets Isaiah and Amos were to appear in our midst, would they accept the corruption in high places, the indifferent way in which the sick, the poor, and the old are treated? Would they condone the indifference to gun control legislation that has allowed some of the finest of our national leaders to be shot dead? Would not our prophets be standing with those who protest against the war in Vietnam, the decay of our cities, the hypocrisy and falsehood that surround our present administration, even at the highest levels?[33]

Sad to say, the identical questions could be raised today that Heschel was raising back in 1972.

After the first mobilization of Clergy and Laity Concerned in Washington in January 1967, a group of us, including Heschel, Michael Novak, and myself, had an hour in the Pentagon with Robert McNamara. As Michael and I flew back to Stanford that night (we were colleagues in Religious Studies) we discovered that we had both had the same reaction: McNamara had been saying to us indirectly, but, we felt, clearly, that the religious leaders had an obligation to create a climate of opinion that would make it politically feasible for the administration to de-escalate the war without turning the country over to the hawks.

Whether that was a correct impression or not, we decided to collaborate on a small book with such an aim in mind. Since Michael was Catholic and I was Protestant, we already had a running start on boxing the ecumenical compass, and realized that such a venture would be more significant with a Jewish collaborator. Heschel had given a powerful address in Washington the day before (to which I shall refer in closing). Did we, relatively unknown and youthful, dare approach the great man and ask for his partnership? We decided to dare. The next morning I phoned Heschel, outlined our project and asked if he would consider uniting with two younger and less well-known colleagues. His reply was instantaneous: "My friend, I am at

your disposal." Three weeks later we had three manuscripts and 5
months later a book, *Vietnam: Crisis of Conscience*. (I cannot refrain
from commenting in passing that one of the things that would surely
most pain Heschel today, as it pains me, is the subsequent repudiation
by Michael Novak of the shared perspectives that bound us together
in those fearful and fateful days.)

Let me share only a few sentences from Heschel's contribution to
that small book, as examples of the expression of moral outrage:

> Must napalm stand in the way of our power to aid and inspire the
> world?
>
> Our government seems to recognize the tragic error and futility
> of the escalation of our involvement, but feels that we cannot
> extricate ourselves without public embarrassment of such a
> dimension as to cause damage to America's prestige.
>
> But the mire in which we flounder threatens us with an even
> greater danger. It is the dilemma of either losing face or losing our
> soul.
>
> To speak about God and remain silent on Vietnam is
> blasphemous.[34]

At a later point he thunders: "Has our conscience become a fossil? Is
all mercy gone? If mercy, the mother of humanity, is still alive as a
demand, how can we say Yes to our bringing agony to the tormented
nation of Vietnam?"[35] The posture invades even his prayers: "O Lord,
we confess our sins, we are ashamed of the inadequacy of our anguish,
of how faint and slight is our mercy. We are a generation that has lost
the capacity for outrage."[36]

. Abraham Heschel never lost "the capacity for outrage." I recall
one time when he was speaking to one of my Stanford classes during
the Vietnam years. One of the ports for shipping napalm to Vietnam
was at Redwood City, near our campus, and students were often there
picketing. It turned out that one of the men involved in the production
of napalm was a friend of one of my students. Both of them were
Jewish. The student asked Heschel in class what she should say to
him. Heschel appeared stunned that a Jew would be involved in such
deeds.

"Go to him," he said, as nearly as I can reconstruct his words, "and
tell him that if he continues making naplam he forfeits the name of
Jew. Go to him and tell him that if he continues to create such things
he forfeits the name of human being. Go to him and tell him that if he
continues to be part of such inhuman destructiveness he sins against

creation and the Creator. Go to him and plead with him," Heschel concluded with barely concealed trembling of limb, "to repent and ask for mercy while there is still time to do so."

Moral outrage. . . .

A Conviction: "Some are Guilty, All Are Responsible"

It was characteristic of Heschel that he often repeated sentences or even whole paragraphs in different books, if he felt strongly about the matter. There is probably no phrase that occurs more frequently in his writings and speeches than some variant of the phrase, "Some are guilty, all are responsible." We find the theme in *The Prophets*, where a chapter sub-heading reads: "Few are guilty, all are responsible."[37] He indicates how the prophets indict everyone: "Can a mortal man be righteous before God"? (Job 4:17), "For there is no man who does not sin" (1 Kings 8:46), and "Enter not into judgment with Thy servent; for no man is righteous before Thee" (Psalm 143:2), after which he concludes: "Above all, the prophets remind us of the moral state of a people: Few are guilty, but all are responsible."[38]

And we also find the theme in his writing about Vietnam: "We must continue to remind ourselves that in a free society, all are involved in what some are doing. *Some are guilty, all are responsible*."[39]

I feel a little bit about this frequently-recurring phrase as Augustine felt about time: I understand it perfectly well until I have to explain it. Even so, a try must be made. It seems to me that at least Heschel is saying that while there may be degrees of our direct involvement in moral evil, rendering some of us more culpable than others, there is no point along that chain at which any one of us may claim total exemption. Some are directly guilty, for example, of the ongoing humiliation of people of color—they pass anti-racial laws, or they refuse to enforce existing nondiscriminatory laws, or they openly defy existing laws, or they whip up racial antagonism, or they speak and write against minority groups; *some* are directly guilty of such things, but *all* are responsible for their ongoing. The one who acquiesces in the evil done by others is implicated in that evil. The one who remains quiet when the demagogue speaks gives his vote to the demagogue. The one who remains indifferent encourages the voices of hatred. Some of us may be guilty, but all of us are responsible.

Heschel applied this theme not only to race, in the speeches in the '60s from which we have already quoted, and by his presence at Selma, but also, as we have seen, in relation to Vietnam. Those at home who privately deplored the war but did nothing about it were targets for his outrage. We have already heard him say: "To speak about God and remain silent on Vietnam is blasphemous." Those at home who were not guilty of dropping anti-personnel weapons on defenseless children, but were paying taxes, or buying Honeywell stock, or refusing to protest such inhumane actions, were responsible for the actions done by the others.

I think this is central to Heschel's social ethics precisely because it does make ethics *social;* there is no possibility of laying all blame for wrongdoing on someone else, or on some other group. We are all implicated in whatever evil the rest do, particularly when we condone it by our silence. Hear him one more time:

> The war in Vietnam has plunged every one of us into unknown regions of responsibility. I am personally involved in the torment of the people injured in battle on the front and in the hamlets, in the shipping of explosives, in the triggering of guns. Though deaf to the distant cry of the orphaned and the maimed, I know that my own integrity is being slashed in that slaughter.[40]

A Conclusion: The Importance of Not Coming Too Late

Let me close with a reminiscence that captures for me the power of Heschel's approach to social ethics, and really summarizes all that I have been trying to say. He feared, like many of us, that people of conscience would neither speak nor act in relation to Vietnam until it was too late, and in his speech at the first Clergy and Laity Concerned mobilization in Washington, in January 1967, he indicated how this fear of coming too late replicated his boyhood fears when studying Torah at age 7 with a rebbe in Poland. Together they confronted the Akeda, the story of the sacrifice of Isaac. Heschel reconstructs the scene:

> Isaac was on the way to Mount Moriah with his father; then he lay on the altar, bound, waiting to be sacrificed. My heart began to beat even faster; it actually sobbed with pity for Isaac. Behold,

Abraham now lifted the knife. And now my heart froze within me with fright. Suddenly the voice of the angel was heard: "Abraham, lay not thine hand upon the lad, for now I know that thou fearest God." And here I broke into tears and wept aloud.

"Why are you crying?" asked the Rabbi. "You know Isaac was not killed."

And I said to him, still weeping, "But Rabbi, supposing the angel had come a second too late?"

The Rabbi comforted me, and calmed me by telling me that an angel cannot come late.

And then Heschel, lifting his eyes from his manuscript and looking directly into our eyes, concluded:

An angel cannot come late, my friends, but we, made of flesh and blood, we may come late.[41]

I was the next speaker on the program. I have forgotten everything that I said. But I have never forgotten that it is possible to come too late.

Notes

1. In preparing this paper I have drawn in a few instances on my earlier "Abraham Heschel: A Passion for Sincerity," *Christianity and Crisis* 33 (December 10, 1973), 256–259. I also wish to record my special indebtedness to two small books on Heschel: Franklin Sherman, *The Promise of Heschel* (Philadelphia: Lippincott, 1970), and especially Byron Sherwin, *Abraham Joshua Heschel* (Atlanta: John Knox Press, 1979), as well as to a series of unpublished essays on Heschel by Rabbi Morton C. Fierman.

   Two stylistic comments: (a) I do not know where Heschel would stand today on the issue of inclusive language, but I have not felt free to tamper with his prose and delete references to "man," "mankind," etc. Let those upon whose ears such terms grate remember that at the time of Heschel's death the issue of sexist language had barely come on the scene. (b) Remember also that Heschel's references to "Negroes," where today we would say "Blacks," were also written before the terminology had begun to shift.
2. Abraham Joshua Heschel, *The Prophets* (New York: Harper and Row, 1962), p. 271; hereafter cited as *Prophets*.
3. *Ibid.*
4. *Ibid.*, pp. 271–272.

5. John C. Bennett, from an unpublished manuscript.
6. Abraham Joshua Heschel, *God in Search of Man: A Philosophy of Judaism* (New York: Farrar, Straus and Cudahy, 1955), p. 34; hereafter cited as *Search*.
7. *Ibid.*, p. 46.
8. Byron Sherwin, *Abraham Joshua Heschel*, p. 12.
9. *Ibid.*
10. Abraham Joshua Heschel, *The Insecurity of Freedom: Essays on Human Existence* (New York: Schocken Books, 1966), pp. 289–290; hereafter cited as *Freedom*. Cf. Abraham Joshua Heschel, *Maimonides* (New York: Farrar, Straus and Giroux, 1982), p. 243. This later book is a translation by Joachim Neugroschel of *Maimonides: Eine Biographie* (Berlin: Erich Reiss Verlag, 1935).
11. *Freedom*, p. 291. The concluding chapter of *Maimonides* is entitled "Imitatio Dei."
12. *Freedom*, p. 161.
13. Cf. Abraham Joshua Heschel, *Man Is Not Alone: A Philosophy of Religion* (New York: Farrar, Straus, and Young, 1951), p. 129.
14. *Search*, p. 31.
15. Abraham Joshua Heschel, *The Earth Is the Lord's: The Inner World of the Jew In Eastern Europe* (New York: Henry Schuman, 1950), p. 72.
16. *Freedom*, p. 97. That the theme is central to Heschel is indicated by the fact that this quotation is taken (without acknowledgement) from *Prophets*, p. 198.
17. *Freedom*, p. 98.
18. Quoted in Sherwin, *op. cit.*, p. 5, from *Freedom*, p. 36.
19. Quoted in Sherwin, from Abraham Joshua Heschel, "No Religion Is An Island," *Union Seminary Quarterly Review* 21 (January 1966), p. 117.
20. *Freedom*, p. 85.
21. *Ibid.*, p. 101.
22. *Ibid.*, p. 102.
23. *Ibid.*
24. *Ibid.*, quoting from *Prophets*, p. 5.
25. *Ibid.*, pp. 102–103.
26. Abraham Joshua Heschel, *Israel: An Echo of Eternity* (New York: Farrar, Straus and Giroux, 1968), p. 146.
27. *Freedom*, p. 95.
28. Cited in Sherwin, from "A Conversation with Doctor Abraham Joshua Heschel," transcript of "The Eternal Light" program, presented February 4, 1973, by the National Broadcasting Company, p. 13. Heschel was interviewed by Carl Stern, NBC News United States Supreme Court correspondent.
29. *Prophets*, p. 402.
30. *Ibid.*, p. 408.
31. In the above discussion on "moral madness" I have drawn on material in my *Elie Wiesel: Messenger to All Humanity* (South Bend, IN: University of Notre Dame Press, 1983), pp. 210–212.
32. *Freedom*, p. 67.

33. From a letter cited in Sherwin, *op. cit.*, p. 7.
34. Abraham Joshua Heschel, "The Moral Outrage of Vietnam," *Vietnam: Crisis of Conscience*, authored by Robert McAfee Brown, Abraham Joshua Heschel and Michael Novak (New York: Herder and Herder, 1967), 48–61, p. 49.
35. *Ibid.*, p. 56.
36. *Ibid.*, p. 50.
37. *Prophets*, p. 14.
38. *Ibid.*, p. 16.
39. *Vietnam: Crisis of Conscience*, p. 50.
40. *Ibid.*, p. 57.
41. *Ibid.*, pp. 51–52, slightly adapted.

9

Heschel's Significance for Jewish–Christian Relations

EVA FLEISCHNER

We all have our stories to tell about Abraham Joshua Heschel. Allow me to tell one also, a story I received from a friend:

The Jesuit Daniel Kilfoyle was one of the founders of Clergy and Laity Concerned about Vietnam. After the first few meetings he was forbidden by his superiors to remain with the group. Daniel Kilfoyle decided to go to one more meeting, so that he could tell his friends in person why he would not be able to stay with them. Abraham Heschel sat across the table from him as he spoke. When he had finished, Heschel got up, came around to where Daniel was sitting, and embraced him saying: "You are my brother!"[1] In some mysterious way Abraham Heschel, the Jew, respected the Jesuit's decision to obey, and understood his pain.

What was it about Heschel that gave him this capacity for understanding a tradition and discipline that were—at least in this case—quite alien to his own, a discipline which, by the 1960s, even some Catholics had difficulty in understanding and accepting? How was it that, less than 3 months after his death, the Catholic magazine *America* published an entire issue dedicated to Heschel,[2] in which Protestant and Catholic scholars joined with Jewish scholars in paying tribute to Heschel? John Bennett, at the time president of Union Theological Seminary where Heschel had been a Visiting Professor, wrote in that issue that "Abraham Heschel belonged to the whole American religious community. I know of no other person of whom this was so true . . . . He seemed equally at home with Protestants and Catholics."[3] We have all heard the tributes paid him by the Christian theologians at this symposium. Jewish scholars also bear witness to Heschel's impact on Christians. Rabbi Samuel Dresner has written of Heschel's "fraternity with the Christian community."[4] And Rabbi Marc Tanenbaum has claimed that "Americans of all religions and races discovered in Heschel a rare religious genius of penetrating insight and compassion."[5]

How do we explain this extraordinary phenomenon: a Jewish religious thinker, utterly and profoundly Jewish, who touched and affected not just the lives, but the thought of Christian theologians? I hope to throw some light on this question in this chapter, by examining the role which Heschel played in bringing Jews and Christians closer to each other. I shall approach my subject in three parts:

First, I shall examine those writings of Heschel in which he speaks explicitly of the relationship between Judaism and Christianity. To this group belong not only passages that reveal Heschel's remarkable understanding of, and sympathy for, Christianity, but also his trenchant and honest—at times painfully honest—articulation of Christian failure, Christian sin *vis-à-vis* Judaism in the course of history, such as the attempts at forced conversion, the "Teaching of Contempt," and Christianity's role in the Holocaust.

A second section will deal with Heschel's influence on the Second Vatican Council. It is closely related to the first, but I examine it separately because of the historical importance of Vatican II for the religious history of the twentieth century in general, and for Christianity's relationship to Judaism in particular.

In a third and last part, I shall briefly look at Heschel's work more broadly, to see how he has influenced Christianity today. While the theme of this paper—Jewish–Christian reconciliation—will be implicit rather than explicit here, this area may well prove to be Heschel's most enduring and profound impact on Christianity. It can perhaps be seen as the source and wellspring of the first two parts of my paper.

One common thread runs through all three sections: the great-heartedness, the generous, deeply caring figure of Abraham Heschel. His personal impact on Christians—whether on renowned theologians, popes, and cardinals, or on large lay audiences, such as the gathering at the 1969 Milwaukee Liturgical Conference—was as immediate and profound as was the impact of his writings. Or, to put it in a Jewish way: Word and deed were always at one in the life of this holy man.

The Relationship of Jews and Christians Today, and in History

Heschel was profoundly optimistic about Jewish–Christian relations. In a 1966 article in *Jubilee*[6] he spoke of the new atmosphere of mutual esteem that has come about, and rejoiced in the fact that he now had Protestant and Catholic students in his classes. It was an important time for him: He had recently become Visiting Professor at Union Theological Seminary, and his hard work during Vatican II had borne fruit. He saw the ecumenical movement as a new horizon of hitherto-unimagined possibilities. But his optimism was not a facile one. Just as during Vatican II it had taken much faith and perseverance for him to continue to believe that an ancient and often sordid history could be turned around, so too there remained moments of discouragement. Jacob Teshima, a student of his at Jewish Theological Seminary, recalls going for a walk with Heschel right after the Munich massacre. Heschel spoke with anguish: "Oh, how I pray for the peace of Jerusalem. But look at the cool indifference of the world's Christians . . . !"[7] He knew times of discouragement, probably many more than those of which we are aware. But he did not allow them to overcome his hope or to paralyze his efforts to bring Jews and Christians closer to each other.

Heschel's theological impact on Christians is all the more striking because he believed that certain limits must be respected in the dialogue. Thus, he held that Jews and Christians should not discuss the figure of Christ.[8] Christology was out of bounds because Heschel believed that each religion is entitled to the privacy of its Holy of Holies; Judaism too "must always be mindful of the mystery of aloneness and uniqueness of its own being."[9]

If the question of ultimate truth was to be bracketed, what was the ground for Heschel on which Jews and Christians could meet face to face and engage each other in meaningful conversation?

Jews and Christians have much in common, but are also separated. The differences must be explored, along with the vast heritage which they share. Common ground and separation are both necessary and should be affirmed. For each community must retain its identity, while respecting and understanding the other. This means that we must understand what we have in common, as well as what divides us; to slight either would make our conversation meaningless. The question for Heschel was always: How can we talk with each other out of our specific and partly different commitments as Jews and Christians? *Out of* commitment, not *without* commitment.

In every God–human relationship—and this relationship was at the heart of all that Heschel wrote and did—there are four dimensions: creed or teaching; faith or the assent of the heart; law or deed, which concretizes the first two; and the context in which faith is lived-out in history, the community.[10]

We are united in the dimension of the deed by our common concern for safeguarding and enhancing the divine image in our fellow human beings, by building a world where justice and freedom can prevail. There is commonality also in the realm of faith (which for Heschel is always distinct from creed): our awareness of "the tragic insufficiency of human faith,"[11] even at its best, our anguish and pain in falling so far short of the divine command, in being callous and hard-hearted in response to God's invitation. All this unites us.

And what divides us? Creed, dogma. "There is a deep chasm between Christians and Jews concerning . . . the divinity and Messiahship of Jesus."[12] Yet, the chasm need not be a source of hostility. For, "to turn a disagreement about the identity of this 'Anointed' into an act of apostasy from God Himself seems to me neither logical nor charitable."[13] The chasm remains, but we can extend our hands to each other across it, provided we are willing to recognize that doctrine can only point the way; it can never hold fast the mystery of God. The goal of our journey is not doctrine, but faith; along the way, doctrines can serve as signposts, but "the righteous lives by faith, not by creed. And faith . . . involves profound awareness of the inadequacy of words, concepts, deeds. Unless we realize that dogmas are tentative rather than final . . . we are guilty of intellectual idolatry."[14]

The challenge for Heschel was not how to relate to a religious institution different from his own, but rather, to human beings who worship God in another way, "who worship God as followers of

Jesus."[15] Can Jews accept this different way as valid? Can they not just tolerate it, but revere it as holy?

Heschel's answer is an unequivocal Yes (we shall see later that he asks no less of Christians). This Yes is based on two convictions— both, I believe, revolutionary not only 15 years ago, but still today.

The first, strongly held and repeatedly affirmed, is Heschel's belief in religious pluralism; not as an evil necessity of which we must grudgingly make the best, but as a desire, even a delight, of God. "God's voice speaks in many languages, communicating itself in a diversity of intuitions."[16] Why should it not be God's will that in this earthly aeon there be a diversity of religions, a variety of paths to God? Heschel finds no evidence in history that a single religion, for the citizens even of one country, is a blessing. Rather, the task of preparing the Kingdom of God seems to him to "require a diversity of talents, a variety of rituals, soul-searching as well as . . . loyal opposition."[17] In his December 10, 1972 interview with Carl Stern, which was to be his last gift to us, he asked Stern if he would really want all the paintings in the Metropolitan to be alike; or, would the world be a more fascinating place if all human faces were the same? In this aeon, at least, diversity of religion seems to him to be the will of God, with the prospect of all peoples embracing one form of worship reserved for the world to come.[18] It is not diversity of belief that is responsible for today's crisis; we stand on the edge of the abyss "not because we intensely *disagree*, but because we feebly *agree*. Faith, not indifference, is the condition for interfaith."[19]

A second conviction underlies Heschel's belief that respect for each other's differences is both necessary and good: his insistence that religion and God are not identical. Religion is only a means, not the end. It becomes idolatrous when regarded as an end in itself. The majesty of God transcends the dignity of religion.[20] There is only one absolute loyalty in which all our loyalties have their root, and to which they are subservient: loyalty to God, "the loyalty of all my loyalties."[21] God alone is absolute. Everything else, when it becomes its own end, runs the risk of being idolatrous. Hence, it stands under constant judgment and in need of repentance and self-examination.[22] This applies to religion itself and to each particular religion.

The relationship between Jews and Christians which is forged out of our common ground and differences is today threatened by a common crisis. We live in a time when all that we hold most dear is in danger of being lost; moral sensitivity, justice, peace, our whole biblical heritage, the very survival of God's presence in the world.

Because the crisis is universal, Jews and Christians must work together to save the world from destruction, to preserve those values that make life human and worth living. We can hope to succeed only through a joint effort; we need each other, because the task is too overwhelming for each of us alone. Are we ready to face the challenge? This is how Heschel describes our common task: "The supreme issue is today not the *halakah* for the Jew or the Church for the Christian . . . ; the supreme issue is whether we are alive or dead to the challenge and the expectation of the living God. The crisis engulfs all of us. The misery and fear of alienation from God make Jew and Christian cry together."[23] We really have no choice. Either we work together to keep God's presence alive in the world, or we will both be engulfed by nihilism, which Heschel sees as a world-wide counter-force to the ecumenical movement.[24] Because we confront the same dangers and terrors, and stand together on the brink, "parochialism has become untenable . . . . No religion is an island. We are all involved with one another. . . . Today religious isolationism is a myth."[25]

The current need for Jews and Christians to work together is, however, more than a strategic necessity for Heschel; it is rooted in history. We are linked historically, and the destiny of one impinges on the destiny of the other. It has always been so. Even in the Middle Ages Jews lived in only relative isolation and acknowledged that Christianity's spiritual impact on the world was important also to them. Heschel quotes Rabbi Joseph Yaabez, one of the victims of the Inquisition, who blessed God for the faith of Christians:

> The Christians believe in Creation, the excellence of the Patriarchs, revelation, retribution, and resurrection. Blessed is the Lord, God of Israel, who left this remnant after the destruction of the second Temple. But for these Christian notions we might ourselves become infirm in our faith.[26]

And yet, despite such moments of insight and recognition, our history is full of prejudice and bigotry. "This is the agony of history: bigotry, the failure to respect each other's commitment, each other's faith."[27] How can we be cured of our bigotry? How can we learn to rejoice in one another's triumphs rather than each other's defeats? The answer for Heschel lies in the awareness of our common humanity, which for him is never mere humanity. Meeting another human being offers me an opportunity to encounter the divine presence here on earth. In the other's presence I stand on holy ground. Why should this holiness disappear if the other holds religious beliefs that differ from mine? "Does God cease to stand before me? Does the difference in commitment destroy the kinship of being human?"[28]

Heschel again looks to his own tradition for an answer. "The pious of all nations have a share in the world to come and are promised eternal life."[29] Jews must therefore respect the faith of Christians. They must do more. Following the tradition of Maimonides, Jehuda Halevi, and Jacob Emden, they must acknowledge Christianity's positive role in the divine plan of redemption.[30] Because of Israel's mysterious election ("in you shall all the tribes of the earth be blessed"—Gen. 12:3), Judaism has a vital stake in the spiritual life of other peoples, particularly Christians, through whom the message of the living God has spread to the ends of the earth. Unlike some Jewish thinkers who, while acknowledging Christianity's debt to Judaism, see the relationship as a one-way street, Heschel believes that the mother cannot ignore her children.

Heschel demands no less of Christians, however, than he demands of himself and his fellow Jews: genuine acceptance of and respect for Judaism. This implies several "precepts" which Heschel spells out quite clearly. I believe he felt the freedom to do so because they concern the history of Christianity, rather than its central affirmation of faith in Christ.

The first "precept" is: No more mission to the Jews. All attempts to convert Jews must be abandoned, for they are a call to Jews to betray their people's tradition, and proof of the failure to accept Judaism as a way of truth, a way to God, valid in its own right.

Renouncing mission to the Jews requires a major change in the Church's attitude:

> For nineteen hundred years the Church defined her relation to the Jews in one word: Mission. What we witness now is the beginning of a change in that relation, a transition *from mission to dialogue.* . . . We must insist that giving up the idea of mission to the Jews be accepted as a precondition for entering dialogue.[31]

The problem, however, is that many Christians are still not sufficiently sensitive to this issue, and do not understand that "we are Jews as we are men."[32]

Heschel recalls his conversation with Gustav Weigel the night before Weigel's death, in Heschel's study at Jewish Theological Seminary.

We opened our hearts to one another in prayer and contrition and spoke of our own deficiencies, failures, hopes. At one moment I posed the question: Is it really the will of God that there be no more Judaism in the world? Would it really be the triumph of God if the scrolls of the Torah would no more be taken out of the Ark and the Torah no more be read in the Synagogue, our ancient Hebrew prayers in which Jesus himself worshiped no more recited, the Passover Seder no more celebrated in our lives, the Law of Moses no more observed in our homes? Would it really be *ad majorem Dei gloriam* to have a world without Jews?[33]

As I reflected on this passage some time ago, I began to wonder what Weigel had said in reply. Heschel does not tell us. I thought that perhaps Mrs. Heschel would know, so I went to see her. She remembered Heschel coming home late that night very moved by his conversation with Weigel, but did not recall his speaking of the Jesuit's response. So the two of us sat there wondering and talking, and soon we were joined by Susannah Heschel and a friend, who were visiting that Sunday. We read the whole passage aloud, slowly. And suddenly the answer emerged, quite clearly. "We opened our hearts to one another in prayer and contrition and spoke of our deficiencies, failures, and hopes." That was how their discussion began: in prayer and contrition. How could Fr. Weigel's response to what followed have been anything but a profound affirmation of Judaism as Judaism? The four of us, as we sat in the Heschels' living room that sunny Sunday afternoon, felt in agreement, reassured, and at peace.

"Would it really be to the greater glory of God to have a world without Jews?" When presented in such terms, it is difficult to imagine even the most fundamentalist of Christians answering, Yes! But alas, we do not have enough Heschels in the world—men, and women, whose love of their God and people and tradition is so radiant that it is quite obviously sacred, so that it becomes inconceivable to wish it away. Convert Heschel to Christianity? A monstrous idea. It is unlikely that the effort was ever made. Why, then, the profound indignation that resounds in his famous—and to many of us so shocking—statement, made at the time of Vatican II and repeated still in the 1972 Stern interview?: "I'd rather go to Auschwitz than give up my religion." His indignation was, no doubt, rooted in his identification with his people's repeated suffering in the course of history and the fear that, unless Vatican II explicitly renounced mission to the Jews, the indignity and suffering would continue.

Fortunately, Heschel saw signs of hope both among Catholics and Protestants. I shall deal with Vatican II below, but let me quote here a few words in this context: "I must say that I found understanding for our sensitivity and position on this issue on the part of distinguished leaders of the Roman Catholic Church."[34] Some Protestant theologians also had begun to reject publicly missionary activity to the Jews—among them Reinhold Niebuhr and Paul Tillich. At a joint meeting of the faculties of Jewish Theological Seminary and Union Theological Seminary, Niebuhr repudiated Christian missionary activity in part because "the two faiths despite differences are sufficiently alike for the Jew to find God more easily in terms of his own religious heritage" and because "practically nothing can purify the symbol of Christ as the image of God in the imagination of the Jew from the taint with which ages of Christians oppression in the name of Christ have tainted it."[35] This is a reference to what has come to be called the "Teaching of Contempt."[36] Renouncing all such teaching is the second "precept" incumbent today upon Christians who are sincere in their desire to take Judaism seriously.

This is no easy task, for the problem is almost as old as Christianity. Christianity was born of Judaism, but "the children did not arise to call the mother blessed; instead, they called her blind."[37] The original affirmation became repudiation, Jewish faith came to be seen as superseded and obsolete, the new covenant as abolishing and replacing the first. "Contrast and contradiction rather than acknowledgment of roots, relatedness and indebtedness, became the perspective."[38] As we today know so well, this perspective was to have tragic consequences, once Christianity emerged from its initial status of a persecuted minority religion and became linked with the power of the Roman Empire. Heschel is painfully aware of the heavy burden of guilt which Christianity has incurred *vis-à-vis* Judaism over the centuries, including a share in the Holocaust. In his address at the 1969 Liturgical Conference in Milwaukee he said: "It is with shame and anguish that I recall that it was possible for a Roman Catholic church adjoining the extermination camp in Auschwitz to offer communion to the officers of the camp, to people who day after day drove thousands of people to be killed in the gas chambers."[39]

The first four words of this sentence strike me as truly extraordinary. Heschel speaks here of the failure—the gigantic failure—of a major religious community not his own; yet he uses the word "shame." Are we ever *ashamed* of the sins of others? We may be shocked and scandalized, we may accuse and blame. But we are ashamed only if in some way we feel related to, identified with, these others—if, in other words, they are not totally "other" to us. How are we to explain Heschel's use of the word in this context? It seems to me that, for him, the failure of the church is not simply failure of the church, but threatens faith everywhere; it is a warning to all who would call themselves religious, a sign that we all have lost our ability to be shocked at the monstrous evil all about us. It was this that made Auschwitz possible; we must regain our moral sensitivity. And so he continues, in the very next sentence: "Let there be an end to the separation of church and God . . . , of religion and justice, or prayer and compassion."

The Holocaust raises the issue of the complicity and silence of the churches as no other event in Western history does. This has become a scandal for Jews and, I am glad to say, for many Christians as well. For some Jews, the scandal is so great that they refuse all dialogue—I can understand them. Others are willing to enter into conversation with Christians, but wonder whether Christianity has lost its credibility since Auschwitz. I can understand them also—some Christians have raised the same question. Heschel's reaction, however, appears different to me. Here he is, at the Catholic Liturgical Conference, speaking in very strong terms of the failure of the Roman Catholic Church. Yet his words are not so much an accusation directed at Catholics, but rather a warning to religious people, to religious institutions, everywhere. What could so easily and understandably have become yet another wall between us becomes instead a source of anguish at human frailty, a frailty from which none of us—not Jews, not Christians—are exempt. "We have no triumph to report except the slow, painstaking effort to redeem single moments in the lives of single men, in the lives of small communities. We do not come on the clouds of heaven but grope through the mists of history."[40]

Notice the "we," again a matter of terminology, seemingly small perhaps, yet so significant. Heschel's concern with the plight of being human, with the tragedy of the human condition, cuts across all religious creeds. We are all sinners, Jews and Christians alike. Perhaps it is this awareness, this deep sense of "we-ness", that enables him to refrain from condemning Christians. I at least do not feel condemned as I read him, nor do I feel that my church is condemned by this man—not even when he points to our sins during the Holocaust. Indeed, I have heard some Christians speak much more harshly of Christianity's failure at that time; I have spoken of it much more harshly myself. Is there some deep font of compassion in Heschel for all human creatures, everywhere, without exception, a compassion which is somehow lacking—or at least diminished—in me, in many of us? I am not sure. But I do know that his refusal to condemn is profoundly healing. I believe it is one of his greatest gifts to us as we strive for reconciliation. He was not blind—far from it; he saw more clearly than most of us. Yet he did not judge or condemn. It is as if he suffered with us who have failed. And this, after all, is the literal meaning of "compassion."

"As long as there is a shred of hatred in the human heart, as long as there is a vacuum without compassion anywhere in the world, there is an emergency."[41] And why is there so much hatred and rage? Because we do not know how to repent. But if all are in the same predicament, there is also hope for all. "History is not a blind alley, and guilt is not an abyss. There is always a way that leads out of guilt: repentance or turning to God."[42]

It is typical of Heschel to see the overcoming of hostility, the healing of ancient wounds, as a task for both communities. He calls upon Jews to ponder seriously the responsibility in Jewish history for having given birth to two world religions. The children did not arise to call the mother blessed but, he asks—these are his questions; I would not dare ask—"Does not the failure of children reflect upon their mother? Do not the sharp deviations from Jewish tradition on the part of the early Christians who were Jews indicate some failure of communication within the spiritual climate of first-century Palestine?"[43] Heschel asks this question after centuries of Christian defamation and persecution of Jews: after the Holocaust. . . .

Again in typical fashion, he moves from the problem, the difficulty, the tragedy, to the opportunity, the new possibility, the hope. Christianity's turning away from the ancient and pernicious teaching is only the first stage in a new era of friendship between Christians and Jews. Heschel believes that we live in a uniquely privileged moment of time, when Christians look to Jews with wonder and hope—a fact which confronts Jews in turn with a new challenge:

We Jews are being put to a new test. Christians, in many parts of the world, have suddenly begun to look at the Jews with astonishment. In particular, the attitude of the Christian community in America is undergoing a change. Instead of hostility, there is expectation. . . . Many Christians believe that we Jews carry the Tablets in our arms, hugging them lovingly. They believe that we continue to relish and nurture the wisdom that God has entrusted to us, that we are loaded with spiritual treasures.[44]

Permit me here to quote a brief excerpt from the 1973 French Bishops' *Guidelines for Christians in their Relationship with Jews*, which is proof, I believe, that Heschel's hope was not too sanguine:

> The permanence of this people through the ages, its survival over civilizations, its presence as a rigorous and exacting partner *vis-à-vis* Christianity are a fact of major importance which we can treat neither with ignorance nor with contempt. The Church which claims to speak in the name of Jesus Christ and which through Him finds itself bound, since its origin and forever, to the Jewish people, perceives in the centuries-long and uninterrupted existence of this people a sign, the full truth of which it would like to understand.[45]

This new Christian expectation is a challenge to the Jewish community, a *kairos*. "Here is a unique responsibility. Such occasions come rarely twice. Are we prepared for the test?"[46]

He at least did what he could to meet it. Fritz Rothschild has written that, when asked later why he had let himself become involved with Vatican II, Heschel replied: "The issues at stake were profoundly theological. To refuse contact with Christian theologians is, to my mind, barbarous. There is a great expectation among Christians today that Judaism has something unique to offer."[47]

And so he allowed himself to become involved with Vatican II— "involved" is too weak a word. He gave of himself tirelessly during the Council, to the point of exhaustion at times, on one occasion traveling to Rome for a special audience with Pope Paul VI, literally on the eve of Yom Kippur. Let me at this point move into the second part of this chapter and consider Heschel's role at Vatican II.

Heschel and the Second Vatican Council

It is generally known that Heschel played an important role at Vatican II. Edward Kaplan wrote in 1973: "Heschel's mostly anonymous but fruitful efforts at the Vatican Council to efface the Catholic view of Jews as Christ-killers sought to change the fabric of the Christian soul."[48]

"Fruitful," but "mostly anonymous" describes the situation well. One reason for the relative anonymity of Heschel's efforts is that they took place largely under the aegis of, and in cooperation with, the American Jewish Committee. The detailed history of Heschel's work remains to be written, but we may look forward to a clarification of his role in the near future. On February 23, 1983, at a one-day symposium in memory of Heschel held at the Jewish Theological Seminary, Rabbi Marc Tanenbaum, who had worked closely with Heschel throughout the Council, presented a paper on Heschel and Vatican II.[49] I am deeply indebted to Rabbi Tanenbaum for giving me a copy of his paper and permitting me to draw on it for this symposium. But I shall limit myself to a few highlights.[50]

During the preparatory stage of the Council, Heschel acted as consultant to the American Jewish Committee and other Jewish agencies, which had been asked by Cardinal Bea's Secretariat for Christian Unity to prepare background documentation for whatever statement on the Jews would be presented to the Council. With Heschel's help, three memoranda were submitted to Cardinal Bea. The first two, in the summer and fall of 1961, dealt with various problem areas in Catholic teaching and liturgy. On November 26, a meeting took place between Cardinal Bea, Abraham Heschel, and Zachariah Shuster of the American Jewish Committee. We have a vignette of Heschel on that occasion from a letter sent by Shuster to the New York office of the AJC, dated December 2, 1961: "He was deeply impressed by his experience in Rome. . . . I can testify that he succeeded in creating a rapport with Christians leaders in a way few laymen and even Jewish religious leaders would have done."[51] In a third memorandum, submitted in May 1962, positive recommendations were made. Tanenbaum calls this "not a conventional memorandum. It was pure Heschel."[52] Heschel lamented religious and racial discrimination against any individual and group, calling for respect of the other's faith. He proposed that a new beginning be made with a Vatican Council Declaration that would recognize the "permanent preciousness" of Jews *as Jews*, rather than seeing them as potential converts, and that would expressly repudiate anti-Semitism and the deicide charge.[53] He could hardly have been more outspoken than he was in this memorandum:

> In view of the past historical events which brought great sacrifice and suffering to Jews on account of their faith as Jews and their race, and particularly in view of the fact that anti-Semitism has in our time resulted in the greatest crime committed in the history of mankind, we consider it a matter of extreme importance that a

strong declaration be issued by the Council stressing the grave nature of the sin of anti-Semitism.[54]

The memorandum went on to propose a number of concrete steps to combat anti-Semitism.

In February 1962, the year in which the Council was to open, three of Heschel's books were sent to Cardinal Bea, who warmly acknowledge them "as a strong common spiritual bond between us." The books were *God In Search of Man, Man Is Not Alone*, and *The Sabbath*. Discussion of the Declaration on the Jews was postponed to the second session, scheduled to open in September 1963. In March of that year, Cardinal Bea visited the United States. After presiding over a Catholic-Protestant Colloquium at Harvard, Bea went on to New York for an interfaith dinner in his honor, attended by U.N. officials and political and religious leaders, among them Heschel.[55]

On March 31, 1963, the day before the dinner. Cardinal Bea and two of his staff members met privately with a group of prominent Jewish leaders to discuss the proposed Vatican Document.[56] The meeting was held at the American Jewish Committee (AJC) building and chaired by Heschel. Cardinal Bea had taken the unusual step of responding, in writing, to a series of questions submitted to him beforehand. The questions centered around the deicide charge, the urgent need to combat anti-Jewish teaching, and the desireability of interreligious cooperation. The Jewish participants hoped that Bea's answers, which were refined in the course of the discussion, would form the basic content of Vatican Declaration.[57]

The next evening Heschel addressed the dinner guests gathered in honor of Cardinal Bea.[58] The man who, the day before, had urgently demanded major reforms from the Catholic Church, now spoke in a different voice. Or perhaps it is more accurate to say that the voice heard on this occasion was Heschel's deepest voice, the one heard through all his other voices. No specific demands were now made. Instead, he addressed the common threat faced by all human beings today, the threat of evil, of the darkness all about us, a darkness partly of our own making. For "the gap between the words we preach and the lives we live threatens to become an abyss. How long will we tolerate a situation that refutes what we confess"? he asked, referring to our nuclear stockpiles.[59] (Notice again the "we-ness.") And he went on to speak of the great spiritual renewal inspired by Pope John XXIII, which "already has opened many hearts and unlocked many precious insights."[60]

Pope John died on June 4, 1963, and the second session opened on September 29 under his successor Pope Paul VI, who supported the Secretariat's position with regard to the Jewish people. In response to a front-page article in *The New York Times* of October 17, which described a draft containing all the points outlined earlier by Cardinal Bea, Heschel issued a personal statement in which he welcomed the forthcoming Declaration as "an expression of integrity . . . , inspired by the presence of God . . . . May the spirit of God guide the work of the Council."[61]

The promising beginning that had been made was, however, to be followed by much turbulence and controversy. Despite the support of Pope Paul VI, opposition to the proposed Declaration and pressures on the Secretariat began to mount. On November 23, 1963, Heschel wrote to Cardinal Bea, expressing his deep concern that the theme of conversion of the Jews had been introduced into a new text. A few days later, at the AJC's request, Heschel went to Rome to meet with Msgr. Johannes Willebrands, who promised to bring his views to Cardinal Bea.[62]

The struggle continued and a new version of the draft appeared in a newspaper story shortly before the third session was to open (on September 16, 1964). The original text was watered down, and the hope was expressed for the Jews' eventual conversion. In a statement dated September 3, 1964, Heschel strongly condemned the new version. His harshest criticism was reserved for the theme of conversion, and shows us that he could, if necessary, be sarcastic—a tone which I think was quite alien to him.

> It must be stated that *spiritual fratricide* is hardly a means for the attainment of "fraternal discussion" or "reciprocal understanding." A message that regards the Jews as candidates for conversion and proclaims that the destiny of Judaism is to disappear will be abhorred by Jews all over the world and is bound to foster reciprocal distrust as well as bitterness and resentment. . . . As I have repeatedly stated to leading personalities of the Vatican, I am ready to go to Auschwitz any time, if faced with the alternative of conversion or death. Jews throughout the world will be dismayed by a call from the Vatican to abandon their faith in a generation which witnessed the massacre of six million Jews and the destruction of thousands of synagogues on a continent where the dominant religion was not Islam, Buddhism, or Shintoism.[63]

The situation was so critical that the AJC arranged an audience for Heschel with Pope Paul VI for September 14, 1964, the eve of Yom

Kippur. Despite the great personal inconvenience to him, Heschel felt he must go. The audience lasted 35 minutes. Heschel, who later described the Pope as having been friendly and cordial, argued his position forcefully and left a lengthy theological memorandum with the Pope for submission to Cardinal Bea's Secretariat. I quote only briefly from what, according to Tanenbaum, is an 18-page document:

> Why is so much attention paid to what Vatican II is going to say about the Jews? Are we Jews in need of recognition. God himself has recognized us as a people. Are we in need of a "Chapter" acknowledging our right to exist as Jews? Nearly every chapter in the Bible expresses the promise of God's fidelity to His Covenant with our people. It is not gratitude that we ask for: it is the cure of a disease affecting so many minds that we pray for.[64]

The struggle around the Declaration continued into the fourth session, amid maneuvering in both camps; enough support for the earlier text was marshalled so that the document that was officially approved on October 28, 1965, and which we know as *Nostra Aetate*, did not make any reference to proselytizing. It was greeted with a mixture of relief and regret. It was admittedly a compromise, but was nonetheless seen as making possible a new beginning.[65] There is no doubt that this perspective has indeed been justified by developments that have taken place since then, developments which are greatly indebted to Abraham Heschel.

Recalling the turbulent course of the Council Declaration, Cardinal Willebrands has written of Heschel's work at the Council.

> I vividly remember the contribution which he made to a specific point of the document *Nostra Aetate*. At a certain moment—Fall 1963—there was a rumor (not without some foundation) that the Secretariat for Christian Unity and Pope Paul VI personally had the intention of expressing, in the forthcoming document, in one or the other brief phrase, the hope for the conversion of the Jewish people to Christ at the end of time. Professor Heschel learned of this, made a special trip to Rome, and asked for a special audience with Pope Paul VI. He wanted to call attention to the dangers inherent in the proposal. He told the Pope that any inclusion of the theme of conversion would produce exceedingly negative reactions in Jewish communities, and would nullify the many good things that the document contained. Indeed, all such thoughts were subsequently abandoned.[66]

I owe a different kind of personal recollection to Fr. Thomas Stransky, C.S.P., who was a member of the Secretariat throughout the Council. In a letter dated April 25, 1983, Fr. Stransky told me of his "most memorable 'Heschel–Stransky' tidbit." (Presumably there were others!)

> When Heschel was told of some minor changes that may be forced into the final draft (we weren't talking about those proposed major ones that never did see light), I commented that though the text would be better as it stood, the minor changes would not destroy the substance and main force of the document. Heschel bristled and replied, "For you, they may be *minor*, but remember, for us Jews, just a scratch from the official Roman Catholic Church on our arms quickly causes a flood of fear in our veins." Yes, I've never forgotten that, especially his spontaneous use of the markings-on-the-arm-image![67]

There are the speeches, there are the memoranda. But perhaps the real Heschel emerges with greater vividness in such stories (of which I have uncovered all too few). In these—and in photographs, which convey more than the written word ever can. Mrs. Heschel has shown me some photographs that were taken at the 1963 New York banquet.[68] Several important people are present in these photos, along with Cardinal Bea and Heschel. What jumps out immediately, however, as one looks at these pictures is the total presence to each other of Heschel and the Cardinal. It is as if the rest of the room and people had ceased to exist for them, as if they were aware only of each other. Cardinal Bea is leaning toward Heschel with a smile, and in intense communication. If ever I have seen Buber's "I and Thou" caught visually, here it is.

Let me speak briefly about what I call the aftermath of Heschel's involvement in Vatican II—both from his point of view, and from that of the highest authority in the Catholic Church.

There are several references to Pope John XXIII in Heschel's writings. In the 1966 *Jubilee* article already referred to, Heschel wrote that "Pope John was a great miracle," who captured the hearts of Christians and non-Christians alike through his sheer love of humanity. "With John and the Council hearts were opened—not only windows, but hearts."[69]

Reflecting on the controversy and on his successful attempts to delete any reference to the conversion of the Jews from the Council document, Heschel said in 1967: "The Schema on the Jews is the first statement of the Church in history—the first Christian discourse dealing with Judaism—which is devoid of any expression of hope for conversion. . . . And let me remind you that there were two versions."[70]

What about the Pope who had received Heschel in a special audience 2 days before the third session? Apparently, Heschel's influence on Paul VI had gone far beyond that meeting. In a general audience in Rome on January 31, 1973, shortly after Heschel's death, the Pope reminded the pilgrims that "even before we have moved in search of God, God has come in search of us." The editors of *America*, after quoting the Pope's words, continue:

> It was not these words that caught the attention of the world press, however, but the fact that the subsequently published text of the papal talk cited the writings of Abraham Joshua Heschel as the source of that thought. This citation of the 1968 French edition of *God In Search of Man* was, in the memory of veteran observers of the Roman scene, an unprecedented public reference by a Pope to a writer who was not a Christian.[71]

Finally, an anecdote. Msgr. John Oesterreicher of the Institute of Judaeo–Christian Studies at Seton Hall University has told me that Paul VI on two different occasions mentioned Heschel to the clergy of Milan, and expressed his appreciation for receiving Heschel's books. The source of this information? Abraham Heschel himself, who, Msgr. Oesterreicher said, told him of this with a kind of joyful pride.[72]

Heschel's Influence on Christian Thought

I believe that Heschel's impact on Christianity goes beyond his involvement in the ecumenical movement and his work at Vatican II. I shall summarize it in three brief points.

First: We have already seen that Heschel's books were read by Cardinal Bea and Pope Paul VI. Long before, however, as early as 1951, Reinhold Niebuhr hailed Heschel as a "commanding and authoritative voice . . . in the religious life of America."[73] As the body of Heschel's work grew, so did his influence on Christian theologians. J.A. Sanders has proposed the intriguing thesis that Karl Barth's *The Humanity of God*, published in 1956, was influenced by *God In Search of Man*, published the year before.[74] Whether through personal friendship or his writings—and frequently through both—Heschel affected the very fabric of Christian thought.

Second: Because God was a shattering reality for him, because the world of the Hebrew prophets was uniquely his own, "many Christian thinkers learned that God already was, and had been for a long time, what traditional Christian dogma taught was revealed only in Christ."[75] Precisely because he was steeped in his own tradition, because he was Jewish in every fibre of his being, Heschel was able to mediate to Christians the riches of what is also their biblical heritage. He saw more clearly than some Christian theologians that the battle with Marcion has not yet been won, that all too often the Hebrew Bible still takes second place to the New Testament. He gave a vivid illustration of this from Vatican II, where each morning after Mass an ancient copy of the Gospel was solemnly carried down to the nave of St. Peter's and deposited on the altar. "It was the Gospel only, and no other book."[76] A simple pious practice, or the expression of a still deep-rooted theological view that the Hebrew scriptures are not fully equal to the Christian scriptures? The latter, it would seem, in light of a text Heschel quotes from Karl Rahner, that "ultimately God effected the production of the Old Testament books to the extent that they were to have a certain function and authority in regard to the New Testament."[77] Against such a view Heschel insisted, again and again, that the Hebrew Bible is primary for Christians as much as Jews, because Jesus' understanding of God was the Jewish understanding of God, Jesus' preaching was about Torah and the prophets, and the Christian liturgy is permeated with the psalms. Heschel's conviction is being validated today by the best Christian biblical scholars.[78] We might ask, however, is it really validation of Heschel, or rather Heschel's influence on these scholars?

My last point is closely related to the second. More perhaps than anyone else, Heschel has opened to Christians the splendors of Jewish tradition—of the Bible, the Sabbath, Hasidism, the rich life of Eastern European Jews prior to the destruction, the mystical meaning of Israel, etc. "To encounter him was to 'feel' the force and spirit of Judaism, the depth and grandeur of it. He led one, even thrust one, into the mysterious greatness of the Jewish tradition."[79] Allow me to quote here some words from the guiding spirit of this symposium, Dr. John Merkle. In a letter to me in October, 1982, Dr. Merkle wrote: "Simply by living and teaching as he did, Heschel may have done more to inspire an enhanced appreciation of Judaism among non-Jews than any other Jew in post-biblical times."[80]

These words resonated in me at the time; I had a hunch they were true, but I was then only just beginning my work on this chapter. My research since then has confirmed that hunch. If Dr. Merkle is indeed correct, then this is, I believe, Abraham Heschel's greatest contribution to the reconciliation of our two communities. For I have long been convinced that the greatest hope for achieving this reconciliation, the surest antidote against Christian anti-Judaism, is for Christians to discover the splendor of a Jewish tradition alive today; so profoundly alive that it can give birth to an Abraham Heschel.

Let me close with words which Heschel wrote about another man, a dear friend, Reinhold Niebuhr, at the end of a penetrating critique of Niebuhr's writings on the mystery of evil. The words seem to me to apply also to the man who wrote them:

> His spirituality combines heaven and earth, as it were. It does not separate soul from body, or mind from the unity of man's physical and spiritual life. His way is an example of one who does justly, loves mercy, and walks humbly with his God, an example of the unity of worship and living.[81]

Notes

1. Conversation with Toby Stein, January 1983.
2. *America* 128 (March 10, 1973).
3. John C. Bennet, "Agent of God's Compassion," *America* 128 (March 10, 1973), 205–206, p. 205.
4. Samuel H. Dresner, "The Contribution of Abraham Joshua Heschel," *Judaism: A Quarterly Journal* 32 (Winter 1983), 57–69, p. 57.
5. Marc H. Tanenbaum, "Heschel and Vatican II: Jewish–Christian Relations." Paper delivered to the Memorial Symposium in honor of Abraham Joshua Heschel, The Jewish Theological Seminary, New York City, February 23, 1983; unpublished at the time of this Symposium, p. 4.
6. Abraham J. Heschel, "Choose Life!" *Jubilee* 13 (January 1966), 37–39, p. 38
7. Jacob Y. Teshima, "My Memory of Professor Abraham Joshua Heschel," *Conservative Judaism* 28 (Fall 1973), 78–80, p. 80.
8. Cf. Abraham J. Heschel, "What We Must Do Together," *Religious Education* 62 (March–April 1967), 133–140, p. 140.
9. "No Religion is an Island," *Union Seminary Quarterly Review* 21 (January 1966), 117–134. This address also appears in F. E. Talmage (ed.), *Disputation and Dialogue* (New York: KTAV, 1975), 337–359. All my references from this essay are to the text in Talmadge. The text here referred to occurs on p. 345 in Talmadge.
10. "No Religion is an Island," pp. 347–348.
11. *Ibid.*, p. 348.

12. *Ibid.*, p. 352.
13. Abraham J. Heschel, "The Jewish Notion of God and Christian Renewal," *Renewal of Religious Thought*, Vol. I of *Theology of Renewal*, ed. by L. K. Shook (New York: Herder & Herder, 1968), 105–129, p. 112.
14. Abraham J. Heschel, *The Insecurity of Freedom: Essays on Human Existence* (New York: Farrar, Straus and Giroux, 1966), 168–178, p. 177; hereafter cited as *Freedom*.
15. "No Religion is an Island," p. 349.
16. *Freedom*, p. 182.
17. "No Religion is an Island," p. 353.
18. *Ibid.*, p. 352.
19. Abraham J. Heschel, "From Mission to Dialogue," *Conservative Judaism* 21 (Spring 1967), 1–11, p. 2.
20. Cf. "No Religion is an Island," p. 352.
21. *Ibid.*, p. 356.
22. Cf. "Choose Life!", p. 39.
23. "No Religion is an Island," p. 344.
24. Cf. *Ibid.*, p. 345.
25. *Ibid.*
26. *Ibid.*, p. 346.
27. *Freedom*, p. 180.
28. "No Religion is an Island," p. 347.
29. *Freedom*, p. 182.
30. Cf. "No Religion is an Island," p. 351.
31. "From Mission to Dialogue," p. 9.
32. *Ibid.*
33. "No Religion is an Island," p. 355.
34. "From Mission to Dialogue," p. 10.
35. Quoted in "No Religion is an Island," p. 356.
36. The term was first used in the 1950s by the French historian Jules Isaac. Cf. both his *Teaching of Contempt* (New York: Holt, Rinehart and Winston, 1964) and *Jesus and Israel* (New York: Holt, Rinehart and Winston 1971). The term has in recent years become part of our vocabulary when referring to the history of Christian anti-Judaism.
37. "No Religion is an Island," pp. 350–351.
38. *Freedom*, p. 169.
39. Abraham J. Heschel, "On Prayer," *Conservative Judaism* 25 (Fall 1970), 1–12, p. 6.
40. *Ibid.*
41. *Ibid.*
42. *Freedom*, p. 165.
43. "No Religion is an Island," p. 350.
44. "From Mission to Dialogue," p. 9.
45. Quoted in *Stepping Stones to Further Jewish–Christian Relations*, compiled by Helga Croner (London–New York: Stimulus Books, 1970), p. 60.
46. "From Mission to Dialogue," p. 11.

47. Quoted in Fritz A. Rothschild, "Abraham Joshua Heschel," *Modern Theologians: Christians and Jews*, ed. by Thomas E. Bird (South Bend, IN: University of Notre Dame Press 1967), 169–182, p. 173.

48. Edward K. Kaplan, "The Spiritual Radicalism of Abraham Joshua Heschel," *Conservative Judaism* 28 (Fall 1973), 40–49, p. 41.

49. Marc H. Tanenbaum, "Heschel and Vatican II: Jewish–Christian Relations," as cited above, note 5.

50. For a comprehensive history of *Nostra Aetate*, cf. J. M. Oesterreicher, "Declaration on the Relationship of the Church to Non-Christian Religions," *Commentary on the Documents of Vatican II*, Herbert Vorgrimler, ed. (New York: Herder & Herder, 1968). The pivotal role played by Msgr. Oesterreicher during the Council can be conveyed in two phrases that have been applied to him: Michael Wyschogrod has called him "the floor manager" of the Declaration, and Cardinal Johannes Willebrands "the historian of the Declaration." I am also indebted to Cardinal Willebrands, president of the Vatican's Secretariat for Promoting Christian Unity, and to Msgr. Jorge Mejia, Secretary of the Commission for Religious Relations with the Jews, both of whom graciously responded to my requests for material referring to Heschel's work with the Council and to Fr. Thomas Stransky, C.S.P., who was on the Secretariat's staff during the Council, and one of its best-informed and best-known members.

51. Quoted in Tanenbaum, *op. cit.*, p. 7.

52. *Ibid.*, p. 8.

53. *Ibid.*

54. Quoted in *Ibid.*, p. 9.

55. Cf. *Ibid.*

56. Sometime during this day, or the next, that (then) Msgr. Willebrands visited Heschel in his study at the Jewish Theological Seminary. Letter from Cardinal Johannes Willebrands to Eva Fleischner, April 23, 1983.

57. Cf. Tanenbaum, *op. cit.*, pp. 10–11. Cf. also Augustin Cardinal Bea, "Aspects of a Peaceful Revolution," *Chicago Studies* 5 (1966), p. 129.

58. This address appears under the title "The Ecumenical Movement," in *Freedom*, 179–183.

59. *Ibid.*, p. 179.

60. *Ibid.*, p. 181.

61. Quoted in Tanenbaum, *op. cit.*, p. 12

62. Cf. *Ibid.*, p. 14.

63. Quoted in *Ibid.*, p. 16.

64. Quoted in *Ibid.*, p. 17.

65. Cf. *Ibid.*, p. 21.

66. Letter from Cardinal Willebrands to Eva Fleischner, April 23, 1983.

67. Letter from Fr. Thomas Stransky, C.S.P., to Eva Fleischner, April 25, 1983.

68. One of these photographs appears as the frontispiece in Eugene J. Fisher, *Seminary Education and Christian-Jewish Relations: A Curriculum and Resource Handbook* (Washington, DC: The National Catholic Educational Association, Seminary Department, in cooperation with The

American Jewish Committee and The Secretariat for Catholic–Jewish Relations, National Conference of Catholic Bishops, 1983).

69. "Choose Life!", p. 31.

70. "From Mission to Dialogue," pp. 10–11. Here is the text from the "second version" referred to by Heschel: "It is worth remembering that the Jewish people's union with the Church is a part of Christian hope. For the Church awaits, as the Apostle Paul teaches (cf. Romans 11:25), with undiminished faith and great longing the entrance of this people into the fullness of the People of God, renewed by Christ." In *Judenhass— Schuld der Christen?!*, ed. by W. P. Eckert, E. L. Ehrlich, and Hans Driewer (Essen: 1964), p. 431f. (The original is in German; English translation mine).

71. *America* 128 (March 10, 1973), p. 202.

72. Msgr. John Osterreicher in a conversation with Eva Fleischner, January 1983.

73. Reinhold Niebuhr, "Masterly Analysis of Faith," Review of *Man Is Not Alone, New York Herald Tribune Book Review* 118 (April 1951), p. 12.

74. Cf. J. A. Sanders, "An Apostle to the Gentiles," *Conservative Judaism* 28 (Fall 1973), 61–63, p. 61.

75. *Ibid.*

76. "The Jewish Notion of God and Christian Renewal," *op. cit.*, p. 112.

77. Karl Rahner, *Inquiries* (New York, 1964), p. 56; quoted by Heschel in "The Jewish Notion of God," p. 112.

78. Cf., e.g., Bernhard W. Anderson, "Confrontation with the Bible," *Theology Today* 30 (October 1973), 267–271.

79. W. D. Davies, "Conscience, Scholar, Witness," *America* 128 (March 10, 1973), 213–215, p. 214.

80. John C. Merkle in a letter to Eva Fleischner, October 10, 1982. Cf. John C. Merkle, *The Genesis of Faith: The Depth Theology of Abraham Joshua Heschel* (New York: Macmillan Publishing Co., 1985), p. 23.

81. *Freedom*, p. 147.

Index

Index

WITHDRAWN AMERICAN UNIV I

DATE DUE

MAY 20 90	
BRODART, INC.	Cat. No. 23-221

WITHDRAWN AMERICAN UNIV LIB

3 1194 00312 3985
AMERICAN UNIVERSITY LIBRARY